Gaudí
and *trencadís* mosaic

Text: Mireia Freixa | Marta Saliné
Photography: Pere Vivas | Ricard Pla

© Triangle Postals SL
Sant Lluís, Menorca
Tel. +34 971 150 451
triangle@triangle.cat
www.triangle.cat

Text:
© Mireia Freixa & Marta Saliné
© Jaume Coll. The trencadís jigsaw puzzle

Photography:
© Pere Vivas & Ricard Pla
—
© Masip Estudi de Fotografia, p. 14
© Joan Barjau, p. 48
© Museu Comarcal Salvador Vilaseca, Reus, p. 10
© Private collection of Juan José Lahuerta, p. 40, 50, 62, 70, 148
© Family Güell de Sentmenat, p. 52

Design:
Joan Barjau
Coordination:
Paz Marrodán
Pablo Longoria
Translation:
Mark Waudby

Printed by:
Gráficas Gongraf SL
Printed in Barcelona
11-2018
Registration number: Me 924-2018
ISBN: 978-84-8478-837-9

WORLD MONUMENTS FUND

www. wmf.org
—
American Express
—

Organisations and documentation centres:
Arxiu Municipal d'Esplugues de Llobregat (AMEL)
Servicio de Patrimonio Arquitectónico Local (SCCM-SPAL)
Grup de Recerca en Història de l'Art i del Disseny Contemporani (GRACMON)
Museus de ceràmica d'Esplugues de Llobregat (MEL)
Museo del Azulejo Manolo Safón de Onda
Museo Nacional de Cerámica y Artes Suntuarias «González Martí» de Valencia
—
Acknowledgements:
Ana Atance Camps
Montse Agüero Duran
Vicent Joan Estall i Poles
Mireia Bosch i Prat
Pau Carbó Berthold
Carme Comas Camacho
Roser Vilardell i Tarruella
Marta de Planell i Mas
Manel Diestre Marín
Jordi Griset Moro
Montse Moragas Freixa
Remedios Mundina
Joan Olona i Casas
Carme Perella Cosconera
Eduard Riu-Barrera
Pia Subias Pujadas
Neus Zapata Tena
Raquel Lacuesta Contreras
Xavier Laumain
Mar Leniz
Àngels López Fusté
Ángela López Sabater
Eduard Riu-Barrera
Silvia Vilarroya Olivé
Carme Hosta
Anna Ribas
Juan-José Lahuerta

"Colour is life"
Antoni Gaudí i Cornet

Foreword

In 2014, the Güell gatehouses were included on the World Monuments Watch list to draw attention to Antoni Gaudí's amazing designs and the conservation needs of the site. This led to an inspired look at the gatehouses, their use today, and the importance of Gaudí and Catalonia's home-grown art nouveau, *modernisme*, in Spain and around the world. Most importantly, it led to a renewed appreciation of *trencadís* in Gaudí's body of work.

Trencadís is a Catalan word which literally means 'easily broken' or 'brittle'. It describes the technique developed by Antoni Gaudí to cover the surfaces of his architectural creations and soon became one of the key elements, and the iconic image, of modernisme, the artistic movement that emerged at the end of the 19th century in Spain, at the same time as art nouveau in France and Arts and Crafts in the United Kingdom.

This technique adheres to two key ideas of Gaudí's philosophy: the representation of nature through colour, and cutting building costs, to such an extent that *trencadís* used 'broken' recycled ceramics as its primary raw material. As the text in this book explains, the technique developed by Gaudí consisted of breaking ceramic objects into pieces and rearranging them in different patterns and motifs on different surfaces. He worked with fellow *modernista* artist, Josep Maria Jujol, in the pursuit of the fashionable trend in Europe at the time of applying man-made art to architecture.

Gaudí first used *trencadís* at the Güell gatehouses, one of the first buildings commissioned by Eusebi Güell to test this imaginative young architect. As a result of this work, Güell went on to commission Gaudí to do other projects — Palau Güell, Park Güell, the church at the Colònia Güell — which would eventually be awarded World Heritage status, the first two in 1984, and the last in 2005.

When the World Monuments Fund first became interested in the gatehouses, they were closed to the public and in a poor state of conservation. Subsequently, Barcelona City Council approached the owner of the site, the University of Barcelona, and signed an agreement to restore the gatehouses in exchange for running its visitor programme.

Thanks to support from American Express, the World Monuments Fund developed two projects involving Barcelona and *modernisme* in association with the University of Barcelona. The first project was associated with sustainable tourism, a hot topic in most tourist destinations. *Modernisme Invisible* is a mobile app that gives a broad overview of the movement, from Barcelona's seven most-visited iconic *modernista* landmarks to a hundred or so buildings throughout the city that showcase the outstanding beauty of *modernisme* and often go unnoticed by visitors and locals.

The second initiative is this book, in which Mireia Freixa and Marta Saliné i Perich tell the story of Gaudí and *trencadís*, and the way it evolved through the use of a variety of materials, from household crockery picked out of therubbish, to fragments of discarded glass bottles and ceramic tiles. The book documents the traditional techniques, illustrated with photographs by Pere Vivas, who beautifully captures the art behind Gaudi's unique approach to architectural design.

The commitment of the World Monuments Fund to cultural heritage conservation has ensured that one chapter in the book would be devoted to the preservation of *trencadís*. A number of restoration projects have been criticised by visitors to the sites, who felt their authenticity had been lost by replacing original, damaged fragments with new ceramic pieces, sometimes using a different technique to the original one. To address these issues, the book includes an article by Dr. Jaume Coll Conesa, director of the Museo Nacional de Cerámica y Artes Suntuarias "González Martí" in Valencia regarding the methods used in the restoration of *trencadís* mosaics.

The World Monuments Fund's initiatives, and those of World Monuments Watch in particular, seek to open up a dialogue about heritage, its importance in our lives, and the fact that we are frequently surrounded by sites that enrich our lives but we fail to notice until the need to preserve them becomes apparent. With our many partners and colleagues, we hope this book triggers a similar conversation about Gaudí's inventiveness and the ways *trencadís* enriches Barcelona's streetscape and delights locals and visitors alike, as well as those who can admire this work on the *Modernisme Invisible* app and in this book.

—

The World Monuments Fund was founded in 1965 and is dedicated to advocacy for and the conservation of the world's cultural heritage sites. Throughout its history, the organization has carried out interventions in more than 600 sites in over 100 countries. The WMF has had the privilege of working in Spain since the 1970s and is grateful to its many partners throughout the country. You can learn more about our work at www.wmf.org

WMF would like to thank American Express for supporting the World Monuments Watch and this publication. American Express is the founding sponsor of the World Monuments Watch. To learn more about the philanthropic commitment of American Express, please visit https://about.americanexpress.com/corporate-responsibility

Introduction

Trencadís ceramic mosaic is the most distinctive element of our home-grown art nouveau, *modernisme*, and the architecture of Antoni Gaudí i Cornet (1852-1926). Without this technique, the bench in Park Güell wouldn't exist, and nor would the façade of the Casa Batlló, or the chimneys on the rooftops of the Palau Güell and La Pedrera. But what lies beyond its wonderful expressiveness and beauty? This is a fascinating topic that we will try to unravel in these pages.

We can provide some answers that justify the great success of *trencadís* during the *modernista* period. Firstly, the local tradition of covering walls with coloured tiles: a hygienic and cost-effective resource that had been used in Catalonia and Valencia since the Middle Ages and become widespread since the 18th century. But we should also mention the fact that the architects, designers and manufacturers were perfectly in tune and created top-quality designs that were mass produced for an enthusiastic public. Lluís Domènech i Montaner (1850-1923) and Antoni Gaudí were the two Catalan *modernista* architects who explored the decorative potential of ceramics, mosaic and *trencadís* in greater depth. But it was Gaudí, with his associate Josep M. Jujol i Gibert (1879-1949), who took the technique into a different realm, creating wall coverings the likes of which had never been seen before. Even so, other architects who were their contemporaries, also made an outstanding use of mosaic and *trencadís*, including Gaudí's assistant Francesc Berenguer i Mestres (1866-1914), or Antoni M. Gallissà i Soqué (1861-1903), Josep Puig i Cadafalch (1867-1956), Alexandre Soler i March (1874 -1949) and Antoni de Falguera i Sivilla (1876-1947). In addition to the architects who recognised the expressive potential of this technique, we should also consider the workshops of mosaicists of the calibre of Mario Maragliano Navone (1864-1944), Lluís Bru i Salelles (1868-1952) and Eliseu Querol i Vilarroya (1895-1980).

This book takes an in-depth look at Gaudí's use of *trencadís*, although the first two chapters will explore the historic and cultural context he worked in. It will then look at the different techniques of mosaic and *trencadís*, their functions, and the materials used. The third chapter, which forms the core of the book, analyses the systems Gaudí used to create his mosaics, starting with the gatehouses of the Güell Estate in Pedralbes, where they were applied using the Hispano-Arabic technique of cutting glazed tiles into geometric shapes, breaking them into pieces (the name *trencadís* comes from the Catalan verb '*trencar*', meaning 'to break'), and applying them to the outer surface like a skin. Other breakthroughs can be seen on the chimneys of the Palau Güell, on the façade and roof of the Casa Batlló — where he also experimented with glass *trencadís* —, at the Torre Bellesguard and the church in the Colònia Güell, culminating in the panels of the hypostyle hall and undulating bench in Park Güell, where he worked with Josep M. Jujol to create a visually stunning ensemble that predated the *modernista* aesthetic. The book concludes with a series of chapters that pinpoint the problems with the restoration and conservation of *trencadís* mosaics and look at their current use and abuse.

The big question we have faced when writing this book is to ascertain whether Gaudí was the first person to use this technique. We believe that we can say, in all certainty, that Gaudí reinvented a technique that had been used in the past and created a new, modern formula consisting of reusing discarded pieces of pottery. However, it is Gaudí himself who confirms his new approach to materials and coverings in a conversation with one of his associates, Cèsar Martinell, on 22nd January 1926. They are discussing the completion of the first tower of the Sagrada Família, and Gaudí talks about the mosaic cladding: "The pointed roofs some architects use in their buildings..." (after he had designed the conical turret for the Palau Güell) "... are not eye-catching enough as a result of the poor-quality cladding..." (Martinell, 1951). Martinell defines the pinnacle-shaped turrets as one of Gaudí's great contributions to architecture but he also recognises that their importance is also down to the materials used. The dome above the main drawing room at the Palau Güell that is the centrepiece of the rooftop, which master and pupil refer to, is made from discarded materials, vitrified sandstone from lime kilns, broken up and applied to the roof and made to resemble *trencadís*. This statement highlights the fact that, in his later years, Gaudí acknowledged that he had devised a new formula in the use of architectural cladding.

← Park Güell. Detail of the undulating bench.

Barcelona. Casa Fajol (1912), Josep Graner. ↑

↑ Barcelona. Palau de la Música Catalana (1905), by the architect Lluís Domènech i Montaner. Mosaics by Mario Maragliano. Busts by Eusebi Arnau.

Antoni Gaudí i Cornet
The architect of colour

Antoni Gaudí completed his primary and secondary education in his home town Reus, which was experiencing rapid growth at the time and had a thriving working class and a liberal bourgeoisie. In 1870, the family moved to Barcelona and Gaudí enrolled at the city's recently founded Provincial School of Architecture. In the early 1880s, Gaudí began working with the architect Joan Martorell i Montells (1833-1906), who had a profound influence on his work as well as his way of understanding architecture. Gaudí always considered him his teacher. In the years leading up to the Barcelona Universal Exhibition (1888), Gaudí began working as an architect in his own right and, like the other architects of his time, remained true to an eclecticism we could call "pre-*modernista*", although he always used brickwork in a special way. In his early works — Casa Vicens (1883-1885), the gatehouses to the summer home of his patron Eusebi Güell (1883-1887), and his main residence, Palau Güell (1886-1890), just off La Rambla — the architect combines the use of historic styles with elements of great decorative originality using hitherto unseen building techniques. He gradually abandoned pastiches of different styles to embark on a new experimental search that took as its starting point the constructive forms and principles of the Gothic period which can be seen in the School of Santa Teresa in Barcelona (1886), the Episcopal Palace in Astorga (1887-1894), and the crypt and apse (1984-1900) of his most iconic work: the Sagrada Família. However, Gaudí evolved beyond the Gothic by introducing the parabolic arch, which is the underpinning and underpinned element at one and the same time.

By the early 20th century, Gaudí had become a much-valued architect among Barcelona's bourgeoisie. He built a series of houses in the new centre of the modern city, the Eixample, which showcase the abstract and organic forms of the worldwide art nouveau movement, as seen in the Casa Calvet (1898-1900), while evolving towards ever-freer forms in the Casa Batlló (1904-1906) and the Casa Milà (1906-1912), which was nicknamed La Pedrera (the Catalan for 'quarry'). One of Gaudí's most important works, Park Güell (1900-1914), shows a direct British influence. At the bchest of his patron, he designed a beautiful garden city for the most affluent members of Barcelona's bourgeoisie. Finally, the church at the Colònia Güell (1908-1914) was approached as a small-scale trial run for what was to become his masterpiece: the Sagrada Família. After Gaudí had completed La Pedrera, he worked for a single private client — Eusebi Güell — on two major commissions that were in the pipeline: Park Güell and the church at the Colònia Güell. However, both projects were curtailed in autumn 1914 when they were cancelled by the Güell family. From this time until his death on 10th June 1926, Gaudí devoted himself solely to the Sagrada Família.

From a very young age, Gaudí had shown an interest in the use of ceramic mosaic as a material for cladding. This is revealed in his essay *Ornamentación* (1878), which we will discuss at length in this book and quote from Laura Mercader's edition (Mercader, 2002) or through texts compiled by his associates and followers. This interest prompted him to visit the studios of one of the last craftsmen versed in the ancestral secrets of glazed ceramics, Joan Baptista Cassany i Folguera (¿ -?). Folguera was based in Manises on the outskirts of Valencia, and the trip, which Gaudí undertook in 1887 with Domènech i Montaner, is described by the latter in 1903, in an article written to mark the death of the architect Antoni M. Gallissà (Casanova, 2002).

The durability of ceramics makes them the ideal medium for the application of colour to architecture. The use of a broad colour spectrum is, as we well know, one of the great challenges that faced the architectural theorists of the 19th-century, from Gottfried Semper (1803-1879) to John Ruskin (1821-1897) (Fanelli and Gargiani, 1999) and, of course, the Barcelona architects of the second half of the 19th century. Elies Rogent i Amat (1821-1897), for instance, who was the director of the Barcelona School of Architecture when Gaudí was studying there, made colour the most important element in the decoration of the main assembly hall of Barcelona University (1863-1892), the building that best represented the Barcelona of the day (Freixa, 2018).

← Gaudí, portrait by Pau Audouard, 1878.

MUNDOS

Gaudí trained in the colourist tradition of architecture and wanted to show its full potential. If we look at his entire output, we will see that he always played with the contrast between textures and colours, and sought to apply these principles to his masterpiece: the Sagrada Família. His final design for the Nativity façade was a sea of colour, as seen in a model presented at the 1910 *Salon de la Société Nationale des Beaux-Arts* in Paris. His pupil, Cèsar Martinell, describes Gaudí showing the model to a group of students from the School of Architecture during a tour of the church on 23rd January 1915, and saying: "colour is life" (Martinell, 1951), a sentence that justifies the publication of this book alone.

The keys to understanding the use of *trencadís* in Gaudí's work

It is impossible to know what Gaudí really thought as he was a great genius who left very little written material. We don't want to speculate on potential ideas based on personal hypotheses because the architect's imagination can be interpreted in countless different ways. Moreover, we feel it is more feasible to list the reasons that triggered his interest in mosaic production. Although he wrote his essay *Ornamentación* in his youth, it features a set of ideas that help us understand the principles that prompted him to make such widespread use of ceramics, mosaic and the *trencadís* technique.

The first of his thoughts that we will highlight here concerns their cost-saving potential in architectural projects. This idea could be applied to ceramic *trencadís* as well as embedding stone into the surface. In Gaudí's essay he says: "The output of most modern industries has focused on saving costs on the manufactured objects. Mechanisation has cut costs on manufactured objects but has made labour more expensive. This phenomenon has spread to every area and building has suffered the effects... So, although labour remains costly and needs to be dispensed with, only the processes can make it cheaper; anything else would be an emasculation, not a saving. It all depends on making abundant use of things that are easy to buy and remove, or sparing use of those that are costly to use" (Antoni Gaudí, transcribed by Mercader, 2002).

Furthermore, it is clear that Gaudí used low-cost materials to make mosaics. Ceramics were produced by local factories and they had a lot of surplus stock, consisting of defective firings, ends of range, and out-of-fashion designs. They still served a purpose because they could still provide a watertight covering but were more affordable because the finish wasn't perfect. Nevertheless, we must refute the assertion that Gaudí only used discarded pieces to create his *trencadís* because he also incorporated into his designs ceramics that he had bought or had even commissioned. This can be seen on the bench in Park Güell or at the Casa Batlló, as well as in his invoices that still survive today. At other times he used recycled objects, including plates, cups or glass objects, such as bottle bottoms. Although these kinds of finishes are usually attributed to Josep M. Jujol, they may well have been Gaudí's idea, as we will see later when we discuss the fact that his experimentation with these materials predates his association with Jujol.

In the above quote, he also suggests dispensing with specialised labour, in this case professional mosaicists. Although industrialisation had boosted fast production, these kinds of workers were more costly than they had been in earlier periods. The *trencadís* technique avoids using specialised workshops with the resulting reduction in costs. The system of cutting ceramics into small regular squares, known as tesserae, was too expensive as a method for covering large expanses of wall, like those created by Gaudí in Park Güell, and at the Casa Batlló and La Pedrera, whereas the *trencadís* shards were created with a single blow of a hammer.

Another prevailing idea was considering beauty the same as function: one of the overriding principles of eclectic architecture: "For an object to be truly beautiful its form must have nothing superfluous about it, except for the conditions that make it useful, bearing in mind the material available and the purpose it must serve, which give rise to its overall shape" (Antoni Gaudí, transcribed by Mercader, 2002).

Along these lines, in his inaugural lecture at the Centre d'Estudis Gaudinistes, "The current educational value of Gaudí's work" (1958), Cèsar Martinell described him as "an architect of structural logic and decorative logic". This logic comes together in mosaic as it is a decorative medium used to cover surfaces.

← Park Güell. Details of the cowl over the porter's lodge (above) and the cross surmounting the administrative block (below).

Likewise, Gaudí understands that beauty can be found in the colour that emerges simply from imitating natural forms: "Ornamentation has been, is and will be coloured; nature doesn't give us any monotonously uniform objects. Everything in the plant and animal kingdom, geology and topography has a more or less vivid colour contrast, and this means we have to colour part or all of an architectural feature. This colour may disappear but the passage of time will ensure it has its own beautiful colour of antiquity" (Antoni Gaudí, transcribed by Mercader, 2002).

Ceramics and mosaics make it possible to bring colour to architecture and see it as a living element. *Trencadís* created the desired variations of tone that stemmed from imitating nature. Although the world around us consists of multicellular forms that change colour according to the time of day, the mosaic and *trencadís* skins act like nature itself based on small pieces that represent the cells.

Just like colour, light makes it possible to see volume. The refraction of light also lends a sense of movement. Even when the colour is less perceptible, in the evening or on dull days, light is captured and reflected back, as if the glazed ceramic simulated shards of mirror. Another major contribution was the creation of textures stemming from the contrast between materials. Moreover, the use of ceramics and mosaic in architecture has the added value of being visible from long distances. Gaudí's conversation with Joan Bergós recalls the example of the large *trencadís* coat of arms that was to be placed over the First Mystery of Glory at Montserrat: "Above the Mystery of Glory was to be placed a coat of arms of Catalonia in mosaic, 20 metres high, that would have been perfectly visible from Monistrol" (Bassegoda, 1974).

The other advantages Gaudí saw in the ceramic covering were much more practical: the waterproofing of the covered elements, its durability — particularly if we compare it with a rendered façade —, the endurance of the original colours due to their resistance to damp, as well as its self-cleaning properties allowing dirt to be eliminated when it rains. In conclusion, mosaic and *trencadís* bring, through their fragments, a great flexibility to cover the curved and rounded forms that Gaudí and his fellow *modernistas* were so fond of.

Beyond the ideas he put forward in his writings or words quoted by his followers, Gaudí's *trencadís* contains a series of characteristics that make it unique. These include the importance he gave to the joints, the spaces between the pieces. Gaudí didn't view them as minor spaces that must remain hidden and believed it wasn't necessary to put the pieces in place exactly so the join couldn't be seen. A gap between each piece was permitted to highlight the outlines. He differed in this regard from specialist mosaicists like Lluís Bru, who insisted that the gap between the pieces should be as narrow as possible. Lluís Bru's grandsons, Josep and Lluís, tell a well-known anecdote about an encounter between their grandfather and Gaudí, when the architect said that the fragments should be applied "by the handful". As soon as Gaudí had left the studio, the mosaicist said to his team: "Don't take any notice of him, he doesn't know how to do mosaics" (Saliné, 2015). This was a clear criticism of Gaudí's system compared with the traditional methods used by mosaicists.

We can't talk about the *trencadís* technique without mentioning Josep M. Jujol, an architect closely associated with Gaudí who also had a rich and varied career alongside the maestro. Jujol obtained his architecture degree in 1906, when he was already working with Gaudí, who he had contacted because they came from the same region, the Camp de Tarragona. His interventions can be seen at the Casa Batlló, La Pedrera and, above all, in the hypostyle hall and on the undulating bench at Park Güell. The boldest interventions in the use of *trencadís* are due to him, although he always sought the maestro's permission. If we analyse Jujol's individual work, mosaic never plays a decisive role or is used to cover large expanses. Moreover, throughout his long career, he worked in different fields, in architecture, where he searched for new forms and techniques and explored different typologies, as well as drawing, calligraphy and design.

← Els Pallaresos (Tarragona). Casa Bofarull (1914-1931), Josep M. Jujol.

Mosaic and its offshoot: *trencadís*

The art of fragments to create an indivisible whole

← Vil·la dels Munts (Tarragona). Detail of a Roman floor mosaic (2nd century AD).

Types of mosaic in antiquity

Mosaic is defined as an ornamental system made of small pieces placed side by side. Visually it consists of a surface embedded with materials like stones, marble, glass or fired clay in different colours which can be arranged to create any type of geometrical, figurative or abstract design.

The way the materials are arranged can be summed up by the word *opus*, indicated by the production process or manufacturing system, and is a term that has been used since Roman times. The word *musivum* – mosaic – refers to the world of Ancient Greece and Rome. However, if we go a little further back in time, we find the Greek word μούσα which means 'muse' and immerses us in the idea of beauty and inspiration. It is said that the Romans adopted this word because the art of mosaic was so sublime that it could only be inspired by the muses, which gave rise to the expression *opus musivum* meaning "made by muses". Stricter, less emotive translations would be "mosaic work", "made of mosaic" and "mural work".

The earliest mosaics, known as *opus lithostrotum*, were made of small stones and their imagery was widely used by the *modernistas*. The *opus sectile* created drawings based on large regular forms, usually made of stone and marble, to create specific forms and splashes of colour that evolved into geometric and figurative motifs. These mosaics remind us of the geometrical ones found in the Arab world. Mosaic gradually evolved towards more perfect drawings and, as Pliny the Elder wrote, it developed as an art form that imitated painting, making it everlasting. According to Pliny, in a definition that has come down to us today, "mosaic is a painting made of stone", a perfect system for perpetuating beauty. This principle led to the creation of workshops in the Vatican during the Renaissance and Baroque periods, that rendered masterpieces by great painters as mosaics.

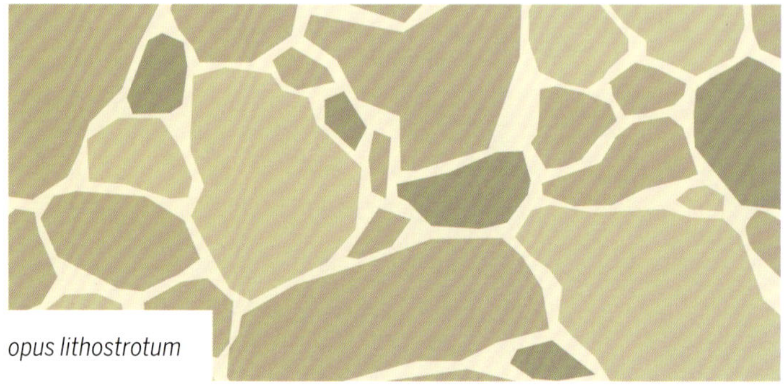

opus lithostrotum

opus sectile

opus tessellatum

opus regulatum

opus vermiculatum

opus musivum

opus segmentatum

opus spicatum

The need for perfection to imitate the brushstrokes of paintings made it necessary to cut stones, glass and ceramics into small pieces called tesserae. Each individual piece, or tessera, has no meaning in its own right; it only has an identity when it is part of a whole — the mosaic — viewed from a distance. Mosaics are generally referred to as *opus tessellatum*, meaning a work made with tesserae, the small square pieces set out in vertical and horizontal lines. However, mosaic production became increasingly streamlined and this led to different shapes of tesserae and other ways of arranging them. In the *opus regulatum*, they have the same shape, but are arranged horizontally rather than vertically. The *opus vermiculatum*, follows the outline of the drawing. The *opus musivum* we have already mentioned consists of creating greater movement, rhythm and beauty. The tesserae were placed around the edges following the outline of the motif and filling in the whole background. This was the type of mosaic used to create murals and marked the transition from flooring to wall cladding. The design, form and size of the tesserae, or materials the mosaics were made of, were key and set trends according to the period they were produced in and the requirements of the time. The *opus segmentatum* is highly reminiscent of the disorderly arrangement of *trencadís* designs, whereas the *opus spicatum* found at the Sagrada Família is neat and ordered, like a herringbone motif.

←

Barcelona. Former Viladot pharmacy (1905). Detail of the ceramic mosaic by Lluís Bru.

←

Barcelona. Former J. Budesca umbrella factory (1920). Mosaic attributed to Mario Maragliano.

Mosaic and *trencadís* in Catalan art nouveau, *modernisme*: form and colour for a new architecture

The art of mosaic in *modernisme* was truly unique and incomparable in relation to European mosaics created in the series of styles epitomised by so-called art nouveau. This compendium of ancient techniques that created new mosaics which could be applied to modern architecture gave rise to a wide variety of types that have to be described in order to understand how extraordinarily widespread mosaic was in Catalonia. The modern name was typified by the materials used in mosaic, from stone and marble to glass and ceramics, and can be described and defined from the terminology that appears in the commercial advertising of the mosaicists of the time.

Roman mosaics were created with tesserae made from hard materials, like natural stone and marble, and were mainly used for flooring to take advantage of their durability and resistance to wear and tear. Venetian mosaics were made from coloured pâte de verre imported from Italy. There was a wide variety of colours and qualities, and the higher-end mosaics were made from metallic colours, including gold and silver.

Finally, ceramic mosaic is the most representative type seen in the *modernista* period and gave rise to its offshoot *trencadís*. It established itself as the most widespread technique for creating *modernista* mosaics. Made with glazed tiles and used to cover vertical surfaces, initially in advertising, it was called Arabic mosaic, but became so popular that the mosaicists themselves replaced this name with the generic term ceramic mosaic. It is important to point out, however, that, initially, the most common mosaics were Roman ones for flooring, Venetian mosaics for covering walls, but, in the end, ceramic mosaics took precedence over the Venetian ones because they gave the same results as Italian glass, and were much cheaper.

For its part, *trencadís* differs from ceramic mosaics for a purely technical reason: the way the pieces are cut. This means we refer to ceramic mosaics when the tesserae are cut into regular shapes and sizes, a technique that required a mosaicist's knowledge and skill. However, *trencadís*, which was irregular in shape, didn't require a professional's skill or knowledge, although some workshops did produce *trencadís* works. Nevertheless, we must accept that the frontier between one technique and the other is often hard to define. It must be recognised that *trencadís*, as part of the mosaic family, was considered a minor technique and this means that the name doesn't feature in any advertising of the period.

Stone mosaics — the *opus lithostrotum* of antiquity — don't feature either, despite the fact that they were widely used during the *modernista* period, although few examples survive today. These mosaics were made from pebbles or rough stones and used on floors and vertical surfaces. Gaudí used this technique in many of his works to cover vertical surfaces, in order to give an image of a living architecture that was in motion, and even zoomorphic, resembling real living animals that blended in with their natural surroundings and were created from locally sourced materials. The Torre Bellesguard, Park Güell and Colònia Güell were examples of this type of mosaic. We can also find stone mosaics on the ceiling inside the Casa Roviralta (1903-1913) in Barcelona, which is also known as the Frare Blanc (White Friar) and was designed by the architect Joan Rubió i Bellver, and at the Casa Mauri (1905-1907), in Pobla de Segur, whose façade and garden are decorated using this mosaic technique. Oral testimony mentions that pebbles from the river were used. These pebbles were gathered by women to obtain a small income.

When the use of mosaic was at it peak it led to a combination of a wide variety of forms, creating what came to be known as mixed mosaics (Saliné, 2015). However, of all the techniques used, ceramic mosaic was best adapted to the new *modernista* architecture. The use of *trencadís* was a boon as it became a unique means of expression and allowed ongoing tests to take place leading to modifications in the technique.

Techniques for producing ceramic mosaics and *trencadís*: piece by piece

Ceramic mosaics cannot be understood if we don't describe how they are produced and the way they differ from *trencadís*. The first step in producing a ceramic mosaic involves thinking about its location. The place it was to occupy — floor or vertical surface — dictated the type of mosaic and materials to be used.

The second step was to make the tesserae based on the type of material required. The hardest materials — marble and stone — were cut with a circular saw that ate away the edges of the material when it was lowered. There were non-mechanical systems for cutting soft materials. The glass used came in the different formats that originated in Italy: flat slabs, and small tesserae, measuring 1.5 × 1 cm and 0.5 cm thick, obtained with tile nippers.

There were countless ways of cutting ceramics and many mosaicists invented their own tools and systems to make them easier to cut. The slowest method involved scoring the glazed side of the tile with a glass cutter and then breaking it with a hammer and chisel, or a grozier, and polishing the edges. The fastest system, used in *trencadís*, involved breaking the tile at random by hitting the unglazed side with a plant pot. We return to the anecdote related by Lluís Bru when Gaudí broke a tile with a plant pot and threw the pieces onto the counter exclaiming: "by the handful, they have to be used by the handful, otherwise we'll never be finished!"

Once the pieces had been shaped, there were two ways of creating the motif on top of the surface. The direct method, which was the system used in antiquity, consisted of applying the tesserae one by one onto wet cement following a design on paper. This system was often used in *modernisme*, usually in rural areas that copied the trencadís design. The formula was widely used by building technicians who knew how to tile. The pieces had to be levelled to avoid any uneven surfaces. At the end of the process, grout was applied to the space between the joints.

The indirect method was the most frequently used method in Italy and was adopted by the mosaicists in the vast workshops at the Vatican in the Renaissance and Baroque eras. The mosaic pieces were stuck on to a life-size drawing on paper. Once the glue had dried, the paper with the tesserae attached was applied to the wall onto a layer of cement (a current comparison would be a sheet of modern mosaic bathroom tiles). When the cement had dried, water was applied to the paper which was peeled off to reveal the mosaic. The joints were then filled in with grout. This method caused a few problems when done with ceramics as the coloured part was attached to the paper meaning the final image couldn't be seen while the mosaic was being worked on, leading to mistakes. To avoid this, mosaicists tried working with tiles glazed on both sides. As has been documented in current restorations, Lluís Domènech i Montaner used these kinds of tiles at the Hospital de Sant Pau and Palau de la Música Catalana. We don't know who came up with this solution. The Lluís Bru Workshop Collection contains some tiles glazed on both sides measuring 15 × 15 cm. The descendants of the mosaicist, Josep and Lluís, attest to the fact that, one day, their grandfather, angry about a botched mosaic, invented this technique. There is also an anecdote about glazed tiles associated with Gaudí. The architect went to place an order for them at the La Esperanza tile works, in Onda, where, according to Remedios Mundina, the granddaughter of the factory owner Francisco Muñoz, they "escorted him off the premises", due to the unusual nature of his order. In truth, the glazed part didn't adhere well and was a poor long-term solution, as contemporary restorations have shown.

The mould-cast mosaic technique was also widely used during the *modernista* period. It proved ideal for creating objects with volume such as jugs and plant pots. Gaudí used plaster half moulds to produce objects that were applied to surfaces using the indirect method. The tesserae were applied to the inner surface of a plaster mould reverse side up and the gaps filled in with cement. This created relief panels which, when turned round, resembled glazed tiles. This system enabled Gaudí and Jujol to produce complex ensembles like the ones at Park Güell.

↑ Park Güell. Medallions on the façade of the administrative block.

Modernista architecture, and Gaudí's work in particular — he loved rounded forms — was the perfect vehicle for mosaics. As they were made with small fragments, they adapted easily to these forms. The gable-shaped tops of buildings, sinuous dados with reliefs, or undulating beaded rings are just some of the countless, beautiful examples of *modernista* architecture.

As far as *trencadís* is concerned, the same word defines the technique. '*Trencadís*' means 'breakable' in Catalan. Although, as we mentioned earlier, commercial advertising didn't feature this technique as it considered it insignificant, it is clearly itemised on the invoices issued by the mosaicists as *trencadís*, or in similar terms. The mosaicist Lluís Bru called it '*mosaico de rotura*' (broken mosaic) or '*mosaico irregular*', as can be seen in the documents about building ceramics held in the Archive of the Esplugues de Llobregat Museum (AMEL).

The *trencadís* technique can be defined as follows:

- It is made with easily breakable materials.
- The technique used to cut the pieces is based on breaking the tiles haphazardly resulting in their irregular shapes.
- The resulting mosaic gives the impression of a surface covering in unequal pieces, placed seemingly at random.

The main difference between *trencadís* and ceramic mosaics lies in the fact that the fragments aren't obtained with care or precision. Their apparent imperfection lends *modernista* architecture its interesting, and unique, dynamism and movement. The forms emerge from the units or splashes of colour (the ceramic shards) and, as a result, the design looks spontaneous, despite the fact that it was almost certainly based on a previous model or idea. The badly cut pieces made this immediate response easier and gave rise to their main characteristic: the great expressiveness and adaptability that stems from the fragments themselves. Although this method of cutting was fast and the pieces could be applied easily, the production technique was really low-tech as the pieces all had to be cut and put in place methodically by hand.

← Casa Batlló. Detail on the main façade.

Other industrial *modernista* techniques also called mosaic

The advertising of the day features other kinds of materials advertised as mosaics. Etymologically speaking, the word mosaic involved a "piece-by-piece" process and, this is why, on many occasions, ceramics, hydraulic and earthenware tiles with their geometric forms were called mosaic. Nevertheless, we believe that there was another intention. The word mosaic conjured up an image of classical techniques and an idea of quality, beauty and richness: virtues that were the undisputed objective of all modern decoration. This is why the word mosaic was often used and its appearance replicated by new industrial manufacturing processes.

The so-called hydraulic mosaics were specially made cement tiles used for interior floorings. The sizes varied from 15 × 15 cm to 20 × 20 cm. They were first manufactured in Catalonia in the late 19th century, and were made with three layers of cement. The upper layer was made of Portland cement, fine marble dust and coloured pigments. To obtain the motifs, the manufacturers used metal plates to separate the colours. They were laid on floors, to make them look as if they were carpeted with a rug. This was achieved by arranging the tiles to form a solid central motif edged with a border. Many of the designs were produced by well-known *modernista* architects and draughtsmen. Butsems & Fradera, Escofet-Tejera y Cª and Orsola Solà y Cª were among the leading manufacturers who achieved great success with these kinds of tiles. Gaudí also used different designs in his projects. Paving stones with a motif in relief were also produced. They were made with a single layer of Portland cement, measuring 4cm thick. We can still see them on city pavements and, from the *modernista* period, at carriage and warehouse entrances. In 1907, Gaudí designed the hexagonal paving stone that can be seen on the pavement along Passeig de Gràcia. Manufactured by Escofet, it was originally designed for the Casa Batlló but was later used at La Pedrera due to the complexity of the design (Griset, 2015).

Barcelona. Casa Lleó Morera (1905), by Domènech i Montaner. Hydraulic-tile flooring in a room on the first floor, manufactured by Escofet. ↑

Earthenware mosaics were made from small, monochrome geometric pieces that were produced industrially and could be glazed at high temperatures. This meant that they were hard enough to be used for indoor flooring. They can be distinguished from the hydraulic tile because they always have geometric forms. They were manufactured by a number of companies, with Casa Nolla, in Meliana, Valencia, and Llevat, in Reus, Catalonia, being among the most important (Laumain, López, 2016). Gaudí used this material in the courtyard on the first floor of the Casa Batlló. The factory *Hijo de Jaime Pujol y Bausis* also produced this type of ceramics, but didn't achieve the success enjoyed by the former two, but we do know that its tiles were used by Josep M. Jujol in the Casa Planells (1924) in Barcelona. The house also has many tiled floors with their corresponding designs found at the AMEL. These hard-wearing tiles were sometimes broken up to create Roman-style *modernista* floors. Their colour palette made it possible to create designs in vivid colours beyond stone and marble.

Both techniques revealed a deliberate desire to be compared — in terms of quality and quantity — with classical mosaics. One such example is the J. Sas Villanueva house, which — as the advertisements described — features tiles that imitated Roman mosaics, and could be applied more quickly due to the industrial process used in their manufacture.

Trencadís was imitated by ceramics, through templates which replicated the shapes of the shards of tile, thereby recreating the impression of *trencadís* fragments.

Fragments and colours were a linking thread throughout the *modernista* period.

↑ Barcelona. Hydraulic paving stones (c. 1907) manufactured by Escofet. Designer unknown.

Casa Milà. Flooring in one of the apartments designed by Gaudí and manufactured by Escofet. ↑

↑ Barcelona. Casa Gabriel Aixelà (1905), Ramon Maria Riudor i Capella. Nolla floor tiles in one of the rooms.

Granada. Alhambra (13th-14th centuries). Tiled wainscot. ↑

Influences on the origins of Gaudí's *trencadís*

But is *trencadís* a new technique? The interest of *modernisme* in mosaics was largely boosted by burgeoning local archaeological studies and the restoration and study of historic ensembles, such as those at Empúries and Centcelles, and those in medieval monasteries, like Santa Maria de Ripoll, restored by Josep Ubach around 1888 (Barral, 1971). Even Josep Puig i Cadafalch remarked on the value of this heritage and lack of studies on preserved landmarks (Puig i Cadafalch, Falguera i Goday, 1909).

Each era when mosaic had been used in the past — Mesopotamia, Egypt, Greece, Rome, Byzantium, and the period spanning Islamic art to the Moorish period — had an influence on *modernista* mosaics. They brought together these techniques to transform them into something completely new.

We should look back again at our classical heritage which features works resembling *trencadís*. These works had a specific name, the *opus segmentatum*, and were used in a more functional, rather than ornamental, type of paving, made with irregular stones of varying sizes. The resulting image was very similar to modern terrazzo floors.

The *modernistas*, and Gaudí in particular, were particularly knowledgeable about the Hispano-Arabic mosaic technique. The beauty of its geometric shapes astonished architects and industrialists who used a great freedom of composition to achieve a milestone in the art of mosaic: a deconstruction of the geometric tiles of antiquity.

Their earliest sources of inspiration were the tiles that covered the walls of Arabic buildings on Spanish territory. They consisted of small regular or irregular ceramic pieces arranged in a decorative pattern to achieve a broad colour palette. The Moorish tradition of embedding small shards of ceramic into cement between bricks comes from the Hispano-Arabic tradition. The technique gives a wonderful contrast between textures and colours. For his part, Luis Gueilburg quotes as a possible forerunner of *trencadís*, the zillij or zillige tiles used in some countries on the southern shores of the Mediterranean which consisted of small pieces of majolica that the artisans broke on their knees and applied with cement (Gueilburg, 2002).

Like the other architects of his generation who had been trained in the eclecticist tradition, Gaudí was well versed in Moorish decorative techniques. In the notebook from his youth he lists the plates featuring Arabic and Moorish architecture in the collection of photographs published by Laurent y Cia, that he had consulted at the School of Architecture library (Mercader, 2002). He would also have seen pictures in colour in the books of chromolithographs, including M. A. Racinet's famous work, *L'Ornement polychrome* (Racinet, undated, plate. XXIX) which was also documented in Barcelona.

One of Gaudí's most direct sources of inspiration were probably the tiled panels on the floor of the cloisters at Poblet Monastery that date from the late 14th century and were still in situ at the time (González Martí, 1952). They were in such a poor state of repair that they were replaced by the flooring we see today, but some original examples remain at the monastery museum, at the Museo Nacional de Cerámica in Valencia and other collections. The panels were set into a base of brick tile and were the work of groups of itinerant Arabic artisans who worked on commissions (Altisench, 1974). Rodrigo Amador de los Ríos wrote the earliest reference to these panels in 1915, although the visit described may have been earlier: "certain very curious framings of tiles that have lost their colour and primitive glaze and can be found on the floor of the main cloisters" (Amador, 1915). They aren't mentioned in the visit to Poblet by the Associació Catalanista d'Excursions Científiques, in November 1875, which is mentioned in its newsletter, *L'Excursionista*. Lluís Domènech i Montaner's monograph about the monastery, written in 1915, doesn't mention the tiles either. All the biographies about Gaudí deal with his fascination at the time with the then abandoned monastery at Poblet. Gaudí may have visited it in his student days as a result of his friendship with Josep Ribera i Sans (1852-1912), a fellow student at the school in Reus who became a prestigious professor in Madrid. Ribera's father was a teacher in L'Espluga de Francolí, a town near Poblet.

Granada. Alhambra (13th-14th centuries). Tiling detail in the Mexuar chamber. ↑

↑ Granada. Alhambra (13th-14th centuries). Tiling detail in the Comares Palace.

Early *modernista* mosaics. From Martorell to Gaudí

The Roman mosaic technique used as flooring was reintroduced to Catalonia in the late 19th century by Italian mosaicists (Voccoli, 2009) as a logical consequence of the development of neo-Gothic architecture in the building of churches. Religious fervour at the time went hand in hand with the idealised Gothic style and the search for new patterns in liturgical art. The furniture, vestments, gold and silver ware and, of course, mosaics, were the perfect companion pieces. In the 1880s, beautiful mosaic floors began to be used in newly built churches. Luigi Pellerin (¿-?) was the first Italian master mosaicist based in Catalonia to use this technique. He was responsible for the floors in the church of the Salesians (1884), designed by Joan Martorell. However, Catalan mosaicists considered Mario Maragliano Navone to be the true maestro among the mosaicists. Navone hailed from a long dynasty of Genoese mosaicists and had settled in Barcelona in 1884, setting up several studios in the city as well as in Madrid. At the turn of the 19th century, Josep Ubach (¿-?) was one of the leading lights of the art of mosaic and had a studio on Carrer de les Corts Catalanes. The beginning of the 20th century saw the emergence of one of the best-known *modernista* mosaicists, Lluís Bru i Salelles, who set up his studio on Carrer Enric Granados in 1904. Eliseu Querol i Vilarroya was another exponent of the ongoing development of mosaic production. He had trained with Maragliano and Bru, and set up his Barcelona workshop on Carrer Dos de Maig in 1914 (Saliné, 2015).

Gaudí wasn't directly involved in the project for the church of the Salesians, but he must have been very familiar with it as it came to fruition at a time when he had a close working relationship with the architect Joan Martorell. Also worth mentioning is the chapel in the shrine above the altar of the Virgin at the basilica of Montserrat, designed and built between 1876 and 1887, by the diocesan architect Francisco de Paula del Villar y Lozano (1928-1901) and his son, Francesc de Paula del Villar i Carmona (1860-1927). The dignified decoration of the chapel was completed with a beautiful mosaic, which is thought to have been done circa 1885. Gaudí had worked as a draughtsman at Montserrat in 1876 (Altés, Baraut, Galobart, 2013), before he graduated and, although he didn't have any contact with the Villars, he must have known about the project.

However, all the authors agree that Gaudí designed the mosaic floor for the church of the sisters of Jesus and Mary (now the parish church of Sant Pacià), in the village of Sant Andreu de Palomar, which is now a borough of Barcelona. The flooring was made between 1879 and 1881 by Luigi Pellerin (Bassegoda, 1989). The church had been designed and built by Joan Torras i Guardiola (1827-1910), but Gaudí was responsible for all the interior design (Voccoli, 2009). We can find a second mosaic design by Gaudí on the floor of the crypt of the Sagrada Família (c. 1883), also made by Luigi Pellerin, and

←

Barcelona. Church of Sant Pacià. Detail (letter Omega) of the Roman-style mosaic floor designed by Gaudí when he was an architecture student.

documented in the religious journal *La Veu de Montserrat*, on 29th December 1888 (Barral, 1971), in spite of the fact that doubts remain whether the current floor is the same one or the result of a subsequent restoration carried out after the Spanish Civil War. In this case, it is likely that the new flooring was made or restored by Mario Maragliano. Both are large-scale projects, as one would expect of such important commissions, and follow the decorative styles practised by the workshops of their teachers: architects of eclectic taste who justified ornamentation by considering it to be the element that gave architecture character and style.

Gaudí made a great leap forward when he used this type of flooring in a residential building, the Casa Vicens (1883-1885). It can be argued that, due to the private nature of the commission, the floors were simpler in design than those in the religious buildings described above, but put the building on the same dignified level. It is important to remember that the Casa Vicens, and the Capricho de Comillas, with their colourful façades covered with ceramic fragments, were the precursors of the technique he honed over the years into a unique process to imbue architecture with colour.

Before we end the chapter, we should mention the tile companies based in Catalonia, as ceramics and mosaics had manufacturing processes in common and produced the raw materials to create *trencadís*. Studies of the ceramics before restoration work took place are the most valuable sources of information — much of the research was carried out by Barcelona Provincial Council — and provide a record of the manufacturers of the day. The most widely documented is the factory Hijo de Jaime Pujol i Baucis, in Esplugues de Llobregat, but there were others, such as Sebastià Ribó and Josep Orriols Pons, and the distributors Ribalaiga Terrés i Mir, and Vda. e Hijos de Juan Vila, all of them based in Barcelona. These are just some of the factories we have records of that produced the ceramics used by Gaudí — either through their catalogues or by the marks on the back of the tiles or the invoices that have survived. Gaudí also placed orders with factories in Valencia, such as La Campana (later known as Peris), La Esperanza, and the stoneware manufacturer Nolla; on the Balearic Islands, with La Roqueta, in Palma; and with the tableware manufacturer Pickman in Seville.

→

Barcelona. Casa Vicens.
Roman-type mosaic flooring on the ground floor designed by Gaudí.

Barcelona. Aisle in the church of Sant Pacià. ↑

↑ Sagrada Família. Detail of the Roman-type mosaic flooring in the central area of the crypt designed by Gaudí.

The development of *trencadís* in Gaudí's work

Step by step, work by work

1.

The turning point: from the Güell gatehouses to Torre Bellesguard

We're going to take a chronological tour of Antoni Gaudí's works to look at the way he gradually introduced ceramic fragments to make them one of the distinguishing features of his work. The technique can be seen for the first time on the dome above the stables and the chimneys of the Güell gatehouses in the district of Les Corts. Here he began using this type of cladding as if it were a multicellular skin, imitating the groups of cells found in nature. The roof of the Palau Güell on Barcelona's Carrer Nou de la Rambla reveals a more mature approach. It was built during the same period as the Güell gatehouses and features eye-catching brick chimneys clad in ceramic and glass *trencadís*, and a dome covered in pieces of vitrified stone left over from lime kilns. Lastly, we will turn our attention to the Torre Bellesguard, which is characterised by the use of stone mosaic, while retaining ceramic and glass *trencadís* elements. The three landmarks can be viewed as early experiments that gave rise to a new method in the art of mosaic, before it became inextricably linked to Gaudí's body of work.

The Güell gatehouses in Les Corts

Breaking down regular geometry

"I have exhausted many of those who have worked with me, in the constant endeavour of improving things. I have not given them my final seal of approval until I have convinced myself I can improve them no further"

Antoni Gaudí (according to Joan Bergós, *Gaudí, l'home i l'obra*, 1954)

Timeline:	**1884-1887**
Developer:	**Eusebi Güell i Bacigalupi**
Location:	**Avinguda de Pedralbes, 7. Barcelona**
Type and use:	**Stables, lunging ring and gatehouses of the Güell estate**

This quote from Gaudí helps us understand that, with the initial use of ceramic *trencadís*, towards the middle of the 1880s, he was beginning to follow a path, steadfastly and tenaciously, in order to attain his major objective: the "perfection" of a project.

No written documents survive about the gatehouses, not even at an official level, as Gaudí didn't apply to the city council for planning permission. Gaudí's first biographer, Josep Francesc Ràfols — who was able to see the architect's papers at the Sagrada Família shortly after his death — dates them at 1887 (Ràfols, 1928), but subsequent bibliography has brought forward the start of building work to 1884, a date that is highly likely due to the complexity of the undertaking.

The wrought-iron gate in the form of a dragon is the best-known and most iconic feature of the Güell gatehouses. It connects two small buildings that had different functions. The one on the left was the porter's lodge, and the one on the right housed the stables, comprising stalls for the horses and a lunging ring. It wasn't the only building Gaudí designed for Güell's estate in Les Corts. Two of the gates to the same property survive, one of them now marking the entrance to the pharmacy faculty and the other behind the biology faculty. In these structures Gaudí also played with the contrast between brick and glazed ceramics but he didn't use *trencadís*. He also built two viewing points, now vanished, that we only know about through old photographs. One of them stood above an unidentified building — possibly a refurbished farmhouse — and the other was attached to a wall on the estate creating a bridge with a parabolic arch. Both structures were decorated with small ceramic pieces similar to those used on the turrets of the gatehouses that we'll describe later, but he doesn't appear to have used *trencadís*.

← A.T.V. Güell gatehouses, postcard, 1905.

The Güells' summer home and garden

In 1859, Eusebi Güell's father, Joan Güell, had purchased a property in Les Corts — Can Custó — and totally refurbished it. The renovations undertaken by Eusebi after he had inherited the estate included a new drive providing faster access from the newly laid out Sarrià road, now the street known as Carrer Manuel Girona, and he commissioned Gaudí to design a new gate and gatehouses. The estate was reached along a private path flanked by twin rows of trees that passed a series of properties and led to the dragon gate. The entrance to the estate was set back from the street so that passers-by wouldn't notice it. This may go some way to explaining the unusual appearance of these buildings.

The dragon gate and the gardens around it have been interpreted as the visual representation of the Garden of the Hesperides described in Jacint Verdaguer's epic poem *Atlantis* (Bassegoda, 1978). Verdaguer had been introduced to the Güell family by Antonio López y López, the marquis of Comillas. He had been chaplain to the marquis who was also Eusebi Güell's father-in-law. Verdaguer completed his poem at the mansion on Güell's estate, called the Torre Satalia, the Catalan for musk rose (*Rosa moschata*). The first edition of *Atlantis* was published in 1878, just five years before Gaudí began working on the estate. The Herculean legend is also depicted at the Palau Güell, the building we will look at next.

The porter's lodge stands on the left-hand side of the gate. It comprises an octagonal central space, which served as a kitchen-cum-dining room, with a dome made in the Catalan vaulting technique consisting of laying flat bricks lengthwise with a space above it to allow air to circulate. On the right-hand side of the gate, are the stables. They consist of two modules — the stalls for the horses, which had a rectangular floor plan with a vaulted roof underpinned by parabolic arches — and a second space designed to be used as a lunging ring, which has a square floor plan and a hyperboloid dome surmounted by a lantern. Gaudí uses an ancient technique — the Catalan vault — in a masterly fashion, resulting in a series of ground-breaking paraboloid and hyperboloid forms. It is also interesting to note that, using the tenets of eclecticism as a starting point, he reworks the principles of Moorish architecture, building brick walls with ceramic details in free-form compositions.

↑

Stone pinnacle depicting the golden fruit from the Garden of the Hesperides. The cement on the brick column below is embedded with small ceramic shards.

Gatehouse façade. →

The exterior. Colour, ceramics and *trencadís*

Gaudí takes a different approach to the ornamentation on the walls and outer walls compared with his two previous projects, El Capricho (1883-1885), in Comillas, and the Casa Vicens (1883-1888), in Barcelona. Until now, his façades were ordered, like a grid, and applied coloured tiles directly onto the wall surface. The decoration was obtained directly from these tiles which were manufactured to order and featured specific decorative motifs: sunflowers in relief in the case of El Capricho, or carnations painted using a stencil at the Casa Vicens. The Güell gatehouses mark a break with this strict aesthetic using new resources. Gaudí put into practice his ideas about multicoloured architecture by highlighting the contrast between exposed brick and the colour of the ceramics, and also introduced *trencadís* which used low-cost, and even recycled, materials. This change in approach marks a shift from an "ornate" architecture to more practical building techniques using simpler materials.

However, not all the coloured elements in this series of buildings are made of ceramics. The main façades feature prefabricated ceramic cladding in a yellowish hue placed above a masonry base reinforced by rows of brick. The interior walls have stuccoed white and red roses (the musk roses described by Verdaguer) set inside circles on a blue background which are, in turn, placed inside circles inside grey and red squares, set between rows of brick.

The walls of the stables and porter's lodge are capped with a brick balustrade in the form of interlocking equilateral triangles. Small ceramic pieces have been embedded into their apexes forming a central point, lending the composition a great sense of colour and order that evokes the Moorish decorative technique and geometry. The small pieces have been cut by a diamond wheel to ensure a clean cut and creating straight, well-finished edges.

↑ Detail of the inner wall with stucco roses.

↑ Balustrade around the walls with perforations in the style of a jalousie. Here Gaudí returned to the simple forms inspired by Arabic art and architecture.

↑ Detail of the gate.

Moreover, on both sides of the dragon gate — the brick column that supports the huge grille and a small entrance for pedestrians — we can see the new resources Gaudí used to apply the ceramic shards. The joints between the bricks are coloured in a unique way by embedding small pieces of ceramic into soft cement using the direct method. The aim is to imbue the entire structure with colour, even the simplest element of all — cement — a material used to join together the parts of a building which here becomes the material used to make the *trencadís* stick.

And Gaudí takes a step further in the decoration of the dome over the lunging ring and the three ventilation chimneys — and to a lesser extent in the air-circulation vent — in the porter's lodge, where *trencadís* is much in evidence. The tile fragments are monochrome and, in some cases, interspersed with splashes of colour, known as *fregalls,* or marbling. The three types of ceramic were very popular during the 19th century and were manufactured on a large scale in Catalonia. They were much cheaper to produce than tiles with painted motifs. The monochrome tiles were simply dipped in pigments to obtain their colour. Those produced using the *fregall* (scouring pad) technique — so named because the pigment was applied directly onto the tile with a wet esparto grass scourer — could be painted in a number of ways and colours. Lastly, the marbling effect imitated top-quality marble with veins created by mixing together watered-down pigments. These types of tile were made at

↑ Gatehouse turrets.

potteries that manufactured everyday materials, such as ceramic skirting, and tiles for kitchens, bathrooms and toilets. These tiles measured 13 × 13 cm or 15 × 15 cm. A new size, measuring 20 × 20 cm, became popular later and was based on the decimal system introduced by the Valencian potteries. It is highly likely that the uptake in the use of these tiles was the result of their lower cost and different available sizes and reflected a change in the tastes of the time.

The jambs of the lantern windows in the dome above the lunging ring are clad in tiles of different shades of green, while the dome itself features triangular motifs filled in with rectangular or triangular mosaics. The irregular shapes, cut into small shards, act as a coloured background that fills in the gaps. However, we can conclude that there is always a dominant regular, ordered geometrical pattern. The monochrome, *fregall* or marbled rectangular and triangular pieces on the ventilation chimneys in the porter's lodge also define the forms and the small shards fill in the gaps.

The Güell gatehouses represent a change of direction in Gaudí's concept of decoration. He moves beyond the Arabic and Moorish technique of embedding walls and banister finials with ceramic pieces, to come up with an ingenious solution in the ventilation chimneys and the dome above the lunging ring: breaking tiles into shards and creating *trencadís* mosaics.

Palau Güell
Functional sculpture

"Everybody makes mistakes, but the one who makes the fewest tries again and again, systematically"

Antoni Gaudí (according to Joan Bergós, *Gaudí, l'home i l'obra*, 1954)

The only visible examples of *trencadís* at Palau Güell are found on the roof, a secondary space not usually seen by visitors to the house. The building can only be understood by viewing it as a whole in which the building, decoration and creation of spaces become a single unit, and every aspect is designed with painstaking attention to detail. When we view the building in this way, the roof also becomes a beautiful and logical element that marks the pinnacle of the building process.

Building a mansion

Eusebi Güell came up with the idea of building a mansion in 1884, when he decided to move from his home at the Palau Fonollar, at 9, Carrer Portaferrissa — next door to the Palau Moja, where the Comillas family lived — and buy a property at 3, Carrer Nou de la Rambla, adjacent to his father's former home just off La Rambla. In fact, the project would join together both properties (González, Lacuesta, 2013). Building work began in the summer of 1886 and the Palau Güell opened officially on the occasion of the 1888 Universal Exhibition, although many of the furnishings and decorations had not been completed.

Timeline:	**1886-1890**
Developer:	**Eusebi Güell i Bacigalupi**
Location:	**Carrer Nou de la Rambla (formerly Conde del Asalto), 3-5. Barcelona**
Type and use:	**Terrace townhouse, extension and refurbishment**
Ceramics:	**Hijo de Jaime Pujol i Bausis, Esplugues de Llobregat; La Campana and La Esperanza, Onda**
	UNESCO World Heritage Site (1984)

← A.T.V. Palau Güell, postcard, 1910.

←
Isabel López Bru.
Palau Fonollar *c.* 1881.
SCCM-SPAL Archive.
Family Güell de Sentmenat Fund. Photographer unknown.

Before going into greater detail about the use of *trencadís* in the building, we need to mention briefly the ceramics found inside. Studies commissioned by Barcelona Provincial Council — the current owner of the building — show that the interior decoration of the Palau Güell contains elements from the refurbishment of the Palau Fonollar (Casamartina, 2017) undertaken by the architect Camil Oliveres i Gensana (1840-1898). Eusebi Güell decided to recover some of the decorative elements from his former home, including parts of the ceramic cladding. The inclusion of these elements didn't pose a problem for Gaudí. Quite the contrary in fact, he is bound to have viewed it as a challenge. Some of the recycled pieces can be seen in an old photo showing Güell's wife in the Palau Fonollar with a ceramic frieze in the background comprising two types of tile with a stencilled motif. From the photo we can deduce that it was taken in one of the main salons of the building, probably on the ground floor, where this type of cladding was commonly used. The recycled materials consist of a series of tiles with a geometric floral motif, which were relaid in the bathrooms and around the washbasin in the library of the new building (Casamartina, 2017). Other elements that may have been reused can be found on the ceiling above the main entrance to the Palau Güell, although we can't rule out the fact that they were bought new. These pieces are decorated with the floral motifs typical of the tiles produced in the 19th century, but measuring 20 × 20 cm — as we mentioned earlier these were the dimensions that were becoming popular about this time — and they were all decorated by stencil, a sign of the ceramic industry's shift towards industrialisation.

The octagonal tiles from the Palau Fonollar that can be seen at the base of the frieze in the photo on the left can now be seen in the gallery on the rear façade of the roof. Their original design has been altered by changing the position of the square around the piece. It is interesting to see the way the tiles have been cut to adapt to the curve of the gallery without changing the geometrical motif. The same tiles were used to decorate the base of a window overlooking the roof. In this case they are framed by a *trencadís* mosaic made with blue marbled and plain white tiles.

A garden of colours and textures on the roof

The roof of the Palau Güell is where we see the *trencadís* technique at its boldest. This part of the house wasn't seen by visitors and was usually kept closed. This means that the *trencadís* on the chimneys was used as a device to bring a touch of colour to the façade, although people had to crane their necks to see them as the street is very narrow. It is well worth the effort as they reveal an innovative contrast between the textures and colours of the façade and the chimneys, especially from the corner of La Rambla. Old photographs also reveal that there was once a wonderful fresco by Aleix Clapés i Puig (1850-1920) on the central façade. According to Lupercio Cruz (2015) the subject would have been Hercules searching for the Hesperides, with scenes either from the first song in Verdaguer's poem *Atlantis*, "The fire in the Pyrenees", or, according to González and Lacuesta (2013), and in our opinion the most likely option, the fifth song "The waterfall" (2013). This vast mural, which revisited the themes of the poem already seen at the Güell gatehouses, must have been extremely striking and made people look at the façade from top to bottom, drawing their attention to the shapes and colours of the rooftop chimneys that rise up like sculptures.

The roof of the Palau Güell is set out on three levels (González, Lacuesta, 2013), with the chimneys and a conical turret rising up in a burst of colour above the city. Each level was given a different name: the rooftop of the maids, where clothes were hung out to dry; the rooftop of the master and mistress; and the viewing point, which was the highest. The turret with its spire stands in the middle of the rooftop of the master and mistress, above the inner drawing room, and served a number of purposes: roof, ventilation and lighting

Chimneys and central lantern on the roof. →

systems, lightning conductor, weather vane and, of course, to lend the building beauty. Gaudí himself, in conversation with Cèsar Martinell (1951), highlighted the importance of the spire that brought new possibilities for covering architectural surfaces, as we pointed out in the introduction to this book. The twenty chimneys are another focal point of the rooftop. Some people count them as eighteen as two of them are joined at the base, and are therefore considered a single unit. In any case, it is important to point out that only eighteen chimneys were envisaged in the initial project submitted to the city council in 1886. This number is also backed up in the plans — a copy of those from 1886 — drawn up in 1910 by Joan Alsina i Arús (1872-1911) and Joan Bordàs Salellas (1888-1961) and presented at the *Salon of the Société Nationale des Beaux-Arts* in Paris that very same year (González, Lacuesta, 2013). We must therefore surmise that two of the chimneys were built after the plans had been submitted: between 1889 and 1890. In their current state, they all have the same volume and shape they did when they were built, but the poor state of repair of the tiles has led to a number of restorations, some of them large scale. However, some of the original pieces remain and these are key to studying the original types of tile used. In order to find out what the tiles looked like before the chimneys were restored, the publication from 1990 (González) is extremely useful. For information about the restoration projects, especially the one carried out in 1992, and their criteria, there are a number of later publications. The most noteworthy being González and Lacuesta's (2013).

It could be said that one of the great virtues of this space lies in the repertoire of materials Gaudí used: a new handbook of textures that served as a basis for ongoing experimentation. Brick was the predominant element and used in abundance as a building material, rather than cladding. What are its similarities to *trencadís*? The way the brick was laid brings to mind the broken pattern of *trencadís*, like a geometric, monochrome fragment that creates a visual unity with the other elements. Six of the chimneys were built with unglazed bricks: five of them are on the rooftop of the maids, and the sixth — which wasn't included in the original plans — on the viewing point.

The exposed-brick chimneys are on the rooftop of the maids, not seen from the street. ↑

↑ The arrangement of the bricks is reminiscent of mosaics.

The chimneys clad in pieces of ceramic tile are the most significant. They feature a large number of recycled materials and, although most of them are just tile fragments, we are still able to see that, unlike the Güell gatehouses, they were mainly created with 20 × 20 cm tiles, rather than the standard 15 × 15 cm ones, some of them applied unbroken directly to the surface. Most of the chimneys are covered in coloured *trencadís*. These were the ones included in the original plans and use tiles from the Palau Fonollar. Another particularly striking one has a base, shaft and cowl covered in pieces of white ceramic tile and porcelain. This model doesn't feature in the initial plans and dates from 1890 (González, Lacuesta, 2013). It was used as the smoke extractor for a fireplace in the sitting room next to Mrs Güell's bedroom, which was also brought from the Palau Fonollar. It is very interesting to see how Gaudí dealt with the use of single colours and used cups to create volume, as well as household crockery made by Pickman. Another chimney is covered with unpolished marble that expands on the idea of a catalogue of materials, embryonic elements that were used in later buildings such as La Pedrera.

Glass used as cladding is another first-time addition to the catalogue of materials referred to above. We can see it on three of the four chimneys placed nearest to the street façade which were restored in 1992. Until then they still retained original fragments on the base and shaft. The shape of the three chimneys adheres to Gaudí's original project but the glass on the cowls is new.

Detail of a *trencadís* mosaic featuring an unbroken tile. ↑

↑ Chimneys clad in ceramic pieces, an early example of *trencadís*.

The mosaics overlooking the main façade are reinterpretations by different artists made for the 1992 restoration. ↑

↑ One of the chimneys is clad in the same materials as the lantern.

Lastly, we wish to draw attention to another innovation: the use of vitrified sandstone that can be seen on the central turret and on one of the chimneys (it is applied to a mainly white base, made of unbroken tiles, which contrasts with the stone on the shaft and cowl). This type of stone was obtained from the left-over materials inside the lime kilns Eusebi Güell had on his estate in El Garraf. These fragments of vitrified sandstone resemble stone mosaics. The sandstone used to make lime disintegrated creating a vitrified layer inside the kilns. This glazed stone provided a highly resistant waterproof layer which was ideally suited to the turret that had to withstand all kinds of weather conditions. Gaudí broke up this material and applied it in pieces directly onto the wet cement. The finish obtained from left-over materials resembled a stone mosaic which had its precursors in Ancient Rome. Rural Roman villas decorated the walls of their garden grottos with stone, like pumice, and the shells of snails and other sea animals, arranging them in a similar pattern to mosaic tesserae. This new technique marked the shift from floor mosaics to wall mosaics (Buenacasa, 2006). We can draw parallels between these mosaics and those created by Gaudí.

There was only a short period of time between the building of the Güell estate and the Palau Güell but it reveals major differences in the concepts behind surface decoration. In the former, the systems used are less risky and more time-honoured. They are made from older tiles, measuring 15 × 15 cm, featuring designs associated with 19th-century models, and were applied more carefully in a more geometric pattern, with particular care being taken over the cut line. However, the major difference lies in the fact that the gatehouses are still redolent of the Moorish tradition, whereas at the Palau Güell, the blend of materials and the originality of the design takes us to another level of creative freedom.

Lantern covered in vitrified sandstone left over from Güell's lime kilns in Garraf. ↑

↑ Detail of the stone *trencadís* on the lantern reminiscent of an organic structure.

Torre Bellesguard

Stone: cladding and natural resource

"Originality consists of going back to the origins; thus, the original is something that returns to the simplicity of the initial solutions"

Antoni Gaudí (according to Joan Bassegoda, *Las conversaciones de Gaudí con Joan Bergós*, 1974)

The Torre Bellesguard (1900-1909) was commissioned by Jaume Figueras' widow, María Sagués, and stands on the remnants of the former palace of the medieval king, Martin the Humane. These archaeological precedents led Gaudí to create a building steeped in symbolism in the *modernista* style but with medieval touches. The fact that few traces of the original palace remain meant that Gaudí could work with absolute freedom.

Stone was one of the main building materials and decorative resources used at Bellesguard. Thus the original materials and early building processes were the fundamental tools to build and decorate the ensemble. However, at Bellesguard, he didn't use left-over materials as he had done with the turret at Palau Güell, choosing to use locally sourced stone instead, to keep costs down and ensure the building blended into the landscape: two aspects he valued so highly. He chose a thin stone with a vein of slate found in the foothills of the Collserola ridge (Vall, 2014), which creates an iridescent effect through its different tones of colour and texture.

Timeline:	**1900-1909**
Developer:	**Maria Sagués, vídua de Figueras**
Location:	**Carrer de Bellesguard, 16. Barcelona**
Type and use:	**Detached House, built on the site of the former palace of King Martin I the Humane, restoration and new build**
Associates:	**Domènec Sugrañes i Gras (1878-1938)**

← Römmler & Jonas. Bellesguard, postcard, 1903.

Gaudí had used natural stone for the first time in the coats of arms on the façade of the Teresian convent school in Barcelona (1888-1890), although, this time, it had no relationship with the landscape. The shields consist of a stone base overlaid with religious symbols in ceramic relief. The stone at Bellesguard was used on all the façades using a technique which, although not exactly a mosaic, performed the same decorative function. The use of half moulds, which we touched on earlier, expanded the possibilities of applying decorative elements, allowing Gaudí to create relief compositions, in this case with stone as the base material. It also enabled him to mould different forms creating a cushion effect. The main door and all the windows are framed by stone placed in such a way as to resemble moulding.

Gaudí used ceramic and glass *trencadís* to decorate the 33-metre-high tower, which is the most important, and visible, part of the building. The base consists of a glass *trencadís* mosaic featuring the four stripes of the Catalan flag, arranged in a spiral, followed by a central section in the shape of a royal crown which forms the base of the cross that indicates the four points of the compass. This lends greater prominence to the *trencadís* technique: it was now given pride of place rather than being relegated to the roof space, with the intention of making it visible from a long distance. The glass shards were applied using the direct method and the colour was painted beforehand on clear glass on the side placed onto the cement. The flag was painted yellow and red, the crown was white and the cross white with red at the ends of each of the four arms. During the 1984 restoration undertaken by Bassegoda (1930-2012), we can still see the traces of the original colours on the cement, despite the fact that almost all the pieces of glass had been lost. On the base, the Catalan coat of arms shows the date the villa was completed (1909), and reveals that, although it had been destroyed on two occasions — in 1652 and 1714 — it had been rebuilt and would never be demolished again (Vall, 2014).

Top of the turret (crown and cross) made of white ceramics and coloured glass. →

Cushion-effect trencadís panels made with stone from the area. →

Venetian-type mosaic with the name of the house embedded into a stone *trencadís* background. ↑

Another important mosaic feature is the small panel above the main door set inside one of the stone cushions which reads "Bell Esguard" (Beautiful View). The panel is made of Venetian glass with a high-quality finish and was almost certainly made at a mosaicist's workshop.

The floor mosaic in front of the entrance can also be attributed to Gaudí. Its functional nature leads us to assume that it is the original one and reminds us of the Portuguese-style mosaics made with large fragments of geometrical stone. Here, Gaudí used locally sourced stone to create simple geometric motifs.

The area around the building was furnished with benches and planters decorated with mosaics made from ceramic tesserae and *trencadís*. They were designed and supervised by the architect Domènec Sugrañes i Gras (1878-1938), who had worked with Gaudí on several projects. Gaudí stopped working on Bellesguard in 1909, but he and Sugrañes had worked together on the building for a number of years beforehand. Sugrañes continued working on the project until 1917 (Subias, 2014). Photographs show that the oldest ceramic benches can be dated between 1902 and 1904 (Subias, 2014).

At Torre Bellesguard, we begin to see different processes and applications that have already broken away from the previous aesthetic. Gaudí used stone from the site and created mosaic and *trencadís* cushions from moulds, incorporated glass as the main material on the façade, and made use of the curve, tying in with the aesthetic tastes of art nouveau. One of the most important aspects is the way a cladding made of fragments encompasses the entire building and, together with the rounded forms, lends coherence to the whole structure, giving an impression of movement. We can interpret the landmark overall as a monumental statue which, seen from the outside, acquires greater perspective due to the arrangement of the viaduct, which was designed by Gaudí himself as an extension of the wall surrounding the estate.

↑ The mosaics on the benches at the entrance were supervised by Sugrañes, while the paving is attributed to Gaudí.

2.
Inventing with each project

We are now going to look at a series of buildings from the period spanning 1900 to 1914, whose influence stretches to 1926, and Gaudí's last masterpiece, the Sagrada Família. The main section of this chapter is devoted to Park Güell, a monumental ensemble showcasing all the surface techniques Gaudí used throughout his career. The project reveals three distinct stages and three very different systems used to apply the *trencadís*. The use of mosaic and tiles on the gatehouse roofs, on the walls and crenellations on the main staircase, and on the wall around the park and the viaducts, predates 1903, and marks the earliest stage. The panels in the hypostyle hall, made between 1907 and 1909, are from the second stage. And lastly, the long, undulating bench, made around 1914, marks the third stage in the building process. From 1907 onwards, Josep M. Jujol made an invaluable contribution to the park and was responsible for creating these extraordinary designs.

Gaudí was working on the Casa Batlló (1904-1906) during the same period. Here the *trencadís* serves as a leitmotif, enveloping the entire building and combining different techniques, textures and colours. In the case of La Pedrera (1906-1912), he used a single colour, breaking with the colour schemes he had experimented with previously. His experiments culminated in the surface finishes at the church at the Colònia Güell, which had a lengthy gestation period (from 1898 until 1914).

In autumn 1914, Gaudí stopped working on the Güell family's commissions and devoted himself entirely to the Sagrada Família. The Sant Bernabé tower was the only one he saw completed in his lifetime. With its beautiful ceramic and glass *trencadís* finish, it is the last example of the architect's trust in this type of cladding.

Gaudí brought his architecture close to nature by creating ensembles that are an integral part of his projects. To achieve this aim, the architecture copies nature and transforms it into one of the main systems to bring them to fruition.

← Park Güell. Detail of the porter's lodge.

Park Güell

Ceramics and glass: colour on the Bald Mountain

"There is no doubt that the distance from which an object has to be viewed involves a composition appropriate to each project"

(Transcribed by Laura Mercader, "La distancia y el punto de vista", in *Antoni Gaudí, escritos y documentos*, 2002)

Park Güell is Gaudí's most ambitious project in terms of his increasing use of ceramics — and *trencadís* — in his architecture. This huge project in the natural landscape constantly breaks the boundaries between the creative act of the artist and architect, and the power of nature. It is important to remember that the dialogue between art and nature has been one of the great questions throughout the history of artistic creativity, a dialogue Gaudí resolves in a dramatic and exceptional fashion by increasing the tension between the two principles.

Timeline:	1900-1914
Developer:	Eusebi Güell i Bacigalupi
Location:	Carrer d'Olot. Barcelona
Type and use:	Residential development and park
Associates:	Josep M. Jujol i Gibert (1879-1949), Joan Rubió i Bellver (1870-1938), Francesc Berenguer i Mestres (1866-1914)
Ceramics:	Peris, Onda (stencil-painted ceramics and monochrome ceramics); Hijo de Jaime Pujol i Bausis, Esplugues de Llobregat (stencil-painted ceramics and monochrome ceramics and elements in relief); Sebastià Ribó, Barcelona; La Roqueta, Palma (the four different-sized discs that were placed on the façade of the Casa Batlló)
Glass:	Tallers Pelegrí (based on testimony by the builder Josep Bayó).
	UNESCO World Heritage Site (1984)

← LB Barcelona. Park Güell, postcard, 1908.

Park Güell, a residential development for affluent families

On 29th July 1899, Eusebi Güell purchased the Can Muntaner de Dalt estate from the marquis of Marianao, Salvador de Samà de Torrents, who, in turn, had bought it from the Larrard family a year earlier. The aim was to build an estate based on the British system of houses set among gardens, hence the name Park, ending in 'k'. The earthworks began shortly afterwards, in October 1900, and, by January 1903, the viaducts and streets, the perimeter wall, the two gatehouses and the staircase with its dragon sculpture, as well as part of the plaza, had been completed. Building work on the hypostyle hall began in 1906 and in March 1909 the ceramic bench around the perimeter of the plaza was begun. In 1914, work came to a standstill when the original development project was deemed a failure. No more houses were built, although the landscaping and other buildings had been completed, with the exception of a chapel that was due to be built on the top of the hill, the Turó de les Menes, but was never begun. Only two houses had been built: the showhouse, designed by Francesc Berenguer, which Gaudí eventually lived in, and the house Martí Trias Domènech commissioned from the architect Juli Batllevell i Arús (1864-1928). For his part, Eusebi Güell had the Larrard's former residence restored and refitted by Gaudí. Standing adjacent to the wide plaza, the house is now a municipal school. Güell's descendants formed a company and sold the estate to Barcelona City Council which opened it as a public park in 1926.

The gatehouses, the perimeter wall, the monumental staircase and the viaducts

The park entrance is flanked by two buildings — the former porter's lodge and the administrative block — and opens onto to a small plaza with a magnificent dragon staircase, that provides a glimpse of the hypostyle hall above with its Doric columns. On entering the park, you have the feeling that you are stepping inside a vast stage set, with two houses on either side with their magnificent timbrel-vaulted roofs covered with ceramic *trencadís*. The east-facing house was the porter's lodge and is surmounted by a whimsical cowl in the form of a toadstool. It resembles the poisonous fly agaric (*amanita muscaria*), and is made with pieces of household porcelain that lend it different tones and textures. The administrative block, which was used by the park residents, has a turret culminating in a four-armed cross, similar to the one Gaudí created at Bellesguard five years later. Many of the ceramic pieces covering the roofs retain their original design, shape and size, but they have become broken over the years. We can also see Gaudí's tendency to use relatively small pieces, arranged in the ordered patterns he had adopted when the roofs were built, before 1903.

Chimney cowl above the porter's lodge. ↑

Turret above the administrative block. ↑

↑ Aerial view of the main entrance, flanked by the administrative block (left) and the porter's lodge (right).

The development stood on an isolated plot of land and, with this in mind, the original plans included a perimeter wall around the entire estate, although only the section along the main entrance was completed. It is a masonry wall capped with alternating red and white ceramic panels interspersed with eye-catching mould-cast medallions containing the words 'Park' and 'Güell'.

Medallions on the wall by the main entrance. ↑

↑ Wall around the estate on Carrer Olot.

Detail of the mullion around the window of the administrative block. ↑

↑ The fragments adapt to the curves of the gatehouse roofs creating a ceramic skin evoking cellular structures.

Trencadís wall by the main staircase. ↑

The small plaza by the entrance leads to a staircase which, in turn, leads to the hypostyle hall and the vast plaza above. The surrounding walls are clad in *trencadís* mosaic panels resembling a giant chess board with large coloured squares and rectangles on a white background. There are terraces above with crenellations covered in strips of coloured *trencadís*. The same types of tile have been used here, with the same motifs, but they have been broken up and rearranged to create new designs.

↑ General view of the twin-flight staircase.

Detail of the wall by the staircase, with concave, white *trencadís* rectangles and convex coloured *trencadís* squares. ↑

↑ Detail of the crenellations on the wall by the staircase.

The staircase consists of three flights of steps with the dragon, or salamander, that has become the park's most iconic image, at the top. The dragon stands above a fountain below which has a *trencadís* medallion bearing the Catalan coat of arms set inside a circle of bluish ceramic shards studded with small circular reliefs. The water spout is in the shape of an animal's head, maybe a dog's. The dragon sculpture has been extensively restored but retains its original colour and shape, except for its claws and almost total loss of its teeth. At the top of the last flight of steps, nestling beneath the hypostyle hall, there is a semicircular bench with a long green strip running round it and relief medallions bearing floral motifs in shades of ochre and red.

The dragon or salamander on the staircase. Above, a detail. ↑

↑ The staircase with the three troughs.

Lastly, we are going to touch on the stone cladding on the viaducts and retaining walls, made in the manner of the Greek and Roman *opus lithostrotum*, similar to the ones we have already seen at the Torre Bellesguard, which Gaudí was working on at the same time as Park Güell. Old photographs reveal that the structures of the viaducts and retaining walls were made using the classic timbrel-vaulting technique covered in rough-hewn stone that creates whimsical *trencadís* shapes. Gaudí sometimes used finishes that simulate smooth ashlars — as is the case of the middle viaduct — although most of them are unpolished stone. Moreover, in some cases, they also adopt beautiful abstract shapes, as is the case with the spirals, resembling large capitals, at the top of the shafts of the columns lining the ramp behind the Casa Güell; the stones that look as if they are falling like rain onto the ramp; the interplay of squares and rectangles, bordered by white pebbles, on the vaulted ceiling of the middle viaduct; or the triangular forms in the upper viaduct. The stones also replicate forms inspired by nature, such as the palm trees on the retaining wall around the edge of the vast plaza, which engage in a dialogue with the real ones planted when work on the park began. The most widespread use of stone mosaic can be seen in the anthropomorphic sculpture of the laundrywoman, so named because she is carrying the tools of her trade, namely a basket on her head containing laundry, and a laundry stick, which had been missing for years and was recently restored. According to oral testimony gathered by Joan Bassegoda in *El Gran Gaudí* (1989), the figure was made by the son of Agustín Massip, who was one of the builders working at the park.

↑ Gaudí dealt with the rough-hewn stone cladding of the viaducts like stone *trencadís* mosaic.

The hypostyle hall: from white *trencadís* to the creativity of Josep M. Jujol

The monumental staircase leads to the hypostyle hall — or hall of columns — which was intended to be the marketplace. It consists of eighty-four fluted columns surmounted by an entablature over which the undulating bench was placed. The hall is covered by small domes built like timbrel vaults and covered with white *trencadís*.

The most eye-catching elements in the hypostyle hall are the soffits, which act as keystones. They are placed in the most spacious areas of the ceiling that were created by removing some of the columns. Josep M. Jujol oversaw the work, which features highly original designs in which ceramics alternate with glass as the main material, as already seen on the chimneys at the Palau Güell, and the cross at the Torre Bellesguard, which was made at the same time. Here, however, there was a meeting of the minds between Gaudí — an architect who wanted to apply a series of unusual materials — , and Jujol, who had a way of expressing himself that was simply out of the ordinary. The result is the extraordinary combination of volumes and colours. According to Carlos Flores, the pair were introduced by Jaume Bayó, the brother of the developer of the Casa Batlló who Jujol had studied under at the School of Architecture in Barcelona (Flores, 2002).

Columns underpinning the hypostyle hall. →

Detail of one of the ceiling soffits in the hypostyle hall. →

The soffits, or medallions, in the centre of the hypostyle hall ceiling feature suns with twenty rays in different colours and textures. They are surrounded by fourteen moons arranged in the manner of ancient keystones. The fact that there are only four suns leads us to assume that there is one for each season of the year. Although they all have the same basic design, the contrast between the colours and materials used in the *trencadís* means each one looks different. The medallions are made of prefabricated brick covered in a wide variety of materials, including glass, pieces of crockery, hydraulic tiles, liquor bottle stoppers, perfume bottles, to create unusual textures. The recent restoration (2016) has returned them to their former splendour. They were certainly made using the direct method, meaning the pieces were applied straight onto the wet cement.

Jujol began incorporating broken-up household crockery, such as plates, soup bowls and glass drinking vessels, into his designs at Park Güell and went on to use them at the Casa Bofarull in the town of Els Pallaresos, in 1914. These elements include plates from the Jujol family's own dinner service (Josep M. Jujol junior, 2017). The park workers were also asked to collect pieces of broken china and other objects and bring them to the site, where they provide a memento of their contribution to the project, almost like fingerprints or signatures.

Suns and moons from the hypostyle hall ceiling. ↑

↑ From left to right and top to bottom, autumn, winter, spring and summer suns.

Detail of the summer sun. ↑

↑ Detail of one of the moons.

The undulating bench: a symphony of textures and colours

The bench-cum-balustrade around the vast esplanade, or artificial plaza, represents the most accomplished use of *trencadís* at Park Güell. One side of the plaza was dug out of the rock and half of it stands directly above the hypostyle hall. What was originally intended to provide a protective balustrade became the undulating bench. The decoration of this extraordinary feature was supervised by Josep M. Jujol from 1910 to 1914 (Duran, 2006; Freixa, Leniz, 2018). However, Jujol's contribution to creating the ceramic bench wasn't acknowledged until the 1970s (Flores, 1974).

The bench structure is made of prefabricated modules of flat brick, like the ones used in the Catalan-, or timbrel-vaulting technique. Each section of the bench is made up of two pieces — the seat and back — held together by an inner metal structure. The modules are concave and convex in shape and arranged in sections of four or eight modules to mimic the rhythmic pattern of the columns in the hypostyle hall below.

We must assume that the mosaic on the bench was done in situ once the modules had been put in place. According to Jujol's son (Josep M. Jujol junior, 1974), his father decorated the backs of each section first and worked on the seat afterwards, but as this is oral testimony, we must treat it with due caution.

Jujol's son also tells us that the architect, a builder and two labourers worked on the bench at the same time. The cartloads of ceramics were left in the middle of the plaza and the pieces chosen to make the necessary compositions. There is a logic behind this process: the work had to be done in situ to cut the costs of moving the pre-assembled sections and pieces to the site (Josep M. Jujol junior, 1974). This on-site workshop system was also adopted by the mosaicists who worked at the Palau de la Música Catalana and the Hospital de la Santa Creu i Sant Pau (Saliné, 2015). There is a curious anecdote about the breakage of pieces where fate may have played a role in the use of *trencadís*. Àngels López i Fusté, the daughter of the draughtsman Francisco López i Sarasa, told us that one day a cart laden with ceramics arrived at the park, and a large quantity of tiles were broken. Eusebi Güell was there at the time and saw the mess, and the waste of money the breakages represented. He was so angry that he protested loudly, but Gaudí told him: "don't worry, this is going to be a work of art".

Unfortunately, we can't verify this information further, but, in any case, the comment leads us to assume that these fragments were going to be a work of art, or would, at least, help create one.

↑ The undulating bench is the pinnacle of the use of *trencadís* at Park Güell.

All the designs for these mosaics were devised and produced in situ as the broken materials were being applied. This led to the involvement of many anonymous helping hands, hence the diversity of the designs. This doesn't mean that the process was completely random: there was probably an initial rough draft but the design came about, and was adjusted, as the fragments were applied. We must also remember that Josep M. Jujol was an extremely accomplished draughtsman. At the School of Architecture in Barcelona he produced spontaneous drawings "Jujol drew very quickly and accurately" (Correa, 1988). He applied this skill to all the projects he worked on with Gaudí. We also know from oral testimony that Gaudí carried out a small trial to test the workers' skills. The ones who showed a knack for decoration were given the task of creating the *trencadís* motifs.

It is highly likely that the spontaneous, abstract, dynamic *trencadís* patterns were planned in advance and not created at random as it may appear at first sight.

The decorative motifs are particularly lavish on the rear of the bench, despite the fact that they can't be seen very easily: around the drainage holes on the front seats we find similar compositions that create very different effects due to the contrasts between the textures and colours. Five billowing stems emerge from each drainage hole. They are set inside a series of different-shaped medallions. These designs reveal a shift towards a freer use of materials with the gradual inclusion of relief fragments and many other different elements, and a certain continuity in the use of medallions with motifs and embedded elements using all kinds of materials.

General view of the rear of the undulating bench. ↑

↑ Detail of the *trencadís* on the rear of the bench.

The front of the bench is divided into two parts: the seat and backrest. The latter contains the richest repertoire of materials. And, as if the rear of the bench wasn't stunning enough, the front features an amazing wealth of designs using different types of *trencadís*, arrangements, sizes and shapes of the fragments. They could be the conceptual forerunners of the 20th-century avant-gardes in their use of collage, and the abstract art and *arte povera* movements.

The half-round mouldings used to separate the seat and backrest were manufactured specifically for the bench, in shades of green, yellow and blue. They are decorated with motifs widely found in everyday glazed pottery — such as household crockery and cooking pots — and in architecture, such as roof tiles. Here these ceramic elements form a continuous line separating the two decorated areas: they are placed strategically at the base of the backrest creating an ergonomic element. The pieces are not cut at right angles but slanted instead to create a zig-zag pattern.

This sinuous structure also acts as a balustrade and roof above the hypostyle hall. ↑

Another row of these half-round mouldings runs along the top of the backrest and prevents water from penetrating the interior of the structure. Jujol and Gaudí established a series of set patterns in the arrangement of the upper and lower rows, which are repeated all the way along the bench, and have been designed to slot in next to each other.

Some of the original half-round mouldings remain in place following restoration work and have another surprise in store: a series of subtle incisions and inscriptions that allude to Jujol's devotion to the Virgin Mary. They were spotted in 1964 by Josep Garganté and Santiago Loperena (Casanelles, 1965), and drawn and described by Joan Matamala (Bassegoda, 1986). Ten years later, Carlos Flores found Jujol's signature among the inscriptions, providing unequivocal proof of the major role he had played in the decoration of the bench (Flores, 1974). The precise, scalpel-like incisions create floral and plant motifs, as well as a crown of thorns. Many of them are accompanied by beautiful calligraphy with words of devotion to the Virgin Mary, written in Latin or Catalan: "Angelus domini nunciavit Maria" (The angel said to Mary), "Tum serveixes" (You serve me), "Amb ella via de pau" (With her the way to peace), "Sos ulls" (Her eyes). There are also references to Christ: "Rex" (King). Jujol's son (1974) reminds us that this devotion to the Virgin was concealed and camouflaged by the different colour patterns on the bench, to ensure it wasn't too visible in a city that, just three years earlier, had gone through a period of great turmoil with the anti-clerical riots of the Tragic Week. The inscriptions are found in the pieces made especially for the bench, and Jujol himself had made the incisions in the wet clay before firing. Gaudí trusted Jujol implicitly in this endeavour, as many first-hand accounts reveal. The fact that the words of devotion to the Virgin had been inscribed on the wet clay leaves us in no doubt that the ceramics had been commissioned and fired while the bench was being built.

The bench-cum-balustrade at Park Güell has become an iconic work that is essential to understanding the concept behind Gaudí and Jujol's architecture: structural innovation combined with extraordinary resources in the application of *trencadís*. It is also the finest of all the collaborations between both architects.

The half-round mouldings were manufactured specifically for the bench. ↑

↑ Many of the half-round mouldings contain inscriptions and drawings.

Park Güell, the largest repertoire of *trencadís* in Catalonia.

There is no doubt that the park contains the largest repertoire of *trencadís* by Gaudí. We mustn't be deceived by the fact that the designs don't seem to follow a geometric approach and appear merely to consist of deconstructing materials. There are extremely precise calculations behind these rounded forms: the chessboard motifs on the main staircase, the mould-cast tiles on the wall tops (like the small crenellations on top of the walls of the staircase and the gatehouse terraces, the panels on the outer walls...) and the half-round mouldings on the bench. Thus, chance is relegated to the breaking up of pieces and the decorative layout of the designs, created by the mosaicists themselves, from Josep M. Jujol to a labourer. However, what we see, above all, is a perfectly calculated geometry, although, in this case, it is hidden.

Gaudí didn't just purchase batches of reject ceramics and glass, although it is clear that he used low-cost industrial materials, as reported by a number of authors and studies performed by Barcelona City Council when it was drawing up the plans for the restoration project (Subias, 1999; 2006; Duran, 2006). In the case of Park Güell, as with many other projects, the ceramics were purchased from the usual suppliers, along with pieces made to order.

The vast repertoire of ceramic *trencadís* at the park can be divided into the following basic types which can create multiple combinations:

- Monochrome *trencadís* with occasional changes of hue.
- Monochrome *trencadís* embedded with other monochrome or multicoloured shapes and abstract designs.
- Multicoloured *trencadís* that breaks an object into one or more pieces and puts them back together to recreate the original design.
- Multicoloured *trencadís* that breaks an object into one or more pieces and puts them back together to recreate a different design.
- Multicoloured *trencadís* that is usually abstract and acts as a background to an element (design or figurative relief) it seeks to embellish.
- Multicoloured *trencadís* that includes everyday objects made with a variety of materials: an example of collage and *arte povera* before they were embraced by the avant-gardes.

14

Monochrome *trencadís* with occasional changes of hue

Upper section of the wall of the entrance. ↑

↑ Ceiling of the hypostyle hall.

Monochrome *trencadís* embedded with other monochrome or multicoloured shapes and abstract designs

Undulating bench. ↑

↑ Undulating bench.

Undulating bench. ↑

↑ Undulating bench.

Multicoloured *trencadís* that breaks an object into one or more pieces and puts them back together to recreate the original design

Crenellations on the staircase (above) and undulating bench (below).

Staircase wall. ↑

↑ Undulating bench.

Multicoloured *trencadís* that breaks an object into one or more pieces and puts them back together to recreate a different design

Staircase wall. ↑

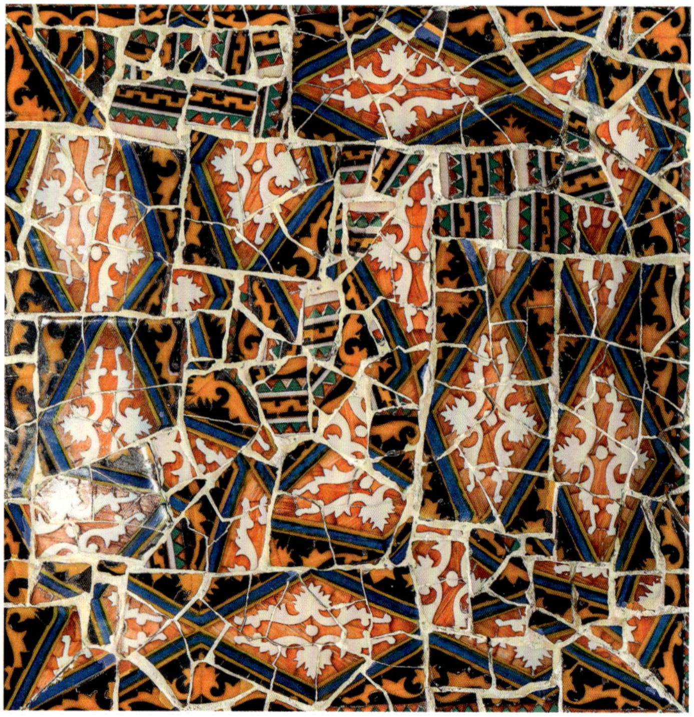

Staircase wall. ↑

Multicoloured *trencadís* that is usually abstract and acts as a background to an element (design or figurative relief) it seeks to embellish

Undulating bench. ↑

Multicoloured *trencadís* that includes everyday objects made with a variety of materials, an example of collage and *arte povera* before they were embraced by the avant-gardes

Undulating bench. ↑

↑ Undulating bench.

↑ Undulating bench.

Casa Batlló

The fragment: unit of the organic element

"The colours used in architecture must be intense, logical and fertile"

Antoni Gaudí (according to Eusebi Casanelles, *Nueva visión de Gaudí*, 1965)

If Park Güell represents a vast repertoire of application techniques, the Casa Batlló is, as a whole, a fragment drawn or applied using *trencadís* and other techniques. Gaudí abandoned his original geometric forms and transformed them into sinuous, rounded designs imitating the colours and forms of nature.

The residential block designed by Gaudí involved the refurbishment of an earlier building designed by Emili Sala Cortés (1841-1921) and built in 1877. The main façade, clad in glass and ceramic shards, is the most striking example from the Catalan art nouveau movement, *modernisme*. The same vertical wall also features glazed ceramic pieces and roundels of different sizes, which alternate with shards of glass. Another interesting aspect of the design lies in the fact that the tops of the windows also replicate the imagery of the façade: stained glass roundels and fragments of glass in different colours and sizes.

Timeline:	**1904-1906**
Developer:	**Josep Batlló i Casanovas**
Location:	**Passeig de Gràcia, 43. Barcelona**
Type and use:	**Residential building, refurbishment**
Associates:	**Francesc Berenguer i Mestres (1866-1914), Josep Canaleta i Cuadras (1875-1950), Domènec Sugrañes i Gras (1878-1938), Josep M. Jujol i Gibert (1879-1949)**
Ceramics:	**La Roqueta, Palma; Nolla, Valencia**
Glass on the façade	**Tallers Pelegrí**
	UNESCO World Heritage Site (2005)

← Casa Batlló, c. 1906. Photographer unknown.

Josep Bayó i Font (1878-1971), the developer who carried out the refurbishment, provided an invaluable first-hand account of the building process in an interview given to Joan Bassegoda i Nonell in 1970 (Bassegoda, 2003). It is now included in the master plan for any future interventions in the Casa Batlló (Onecha, Bosch, Olona, Dotor, 2017). Bayó explains that Gaudí gave instructions “in person” about the main façade, which is covered in coloured glass and ceramic roundels. He adds: “He told us, ‘fill in that hole with a green piece; finish off that tip in green, and that one there in blue’. And as we had already plastered and smoothed out the wall surface, we used grout to apply the section we were going to work on during these two— or four-hour shifts”. Bayó’s description points to a use of the direct method. While the cement was still soft, the shards of glass could be applied and levelled off to make sure they didn’t protrude. Bayó adds that Gaudí always told them: “not to cut the ends of the pieces off ... and to ensure that the glass always ended in a point so it would interlock with the other pieces”. If we think back to the technique used to produce mosaics, the tile pieces had jagged edges so they would fit look like joins. Now Gaudí created the same effect with glass shards that fitted together in a jagged zig-zag pattern. The turret on the façade features the gilded ceramic relief monograms of the Holy Family of Nazareth: in ascending order, they read Joseph (JHP), Mary (M crowned) and Christ (IHS).

Turret on the main façade. ↑

↑ Detail of the main façade with ceramics and glass.

Main façade. Ceramic disc. ↑

↑ Main courtyard. *Trencadís* mosaic on a planter.

The turret is surmounted by an elaborate, bulbous dome, and the four-armed cross is cracked. The cross developed cracks during firing but Gaudí rescued it and used it as a magnificent pinnacle. If you didn't know this anecdote, it might appear that the cross was broken deliberately by the architect. First-hand accounts from the time (Bassegoda, 1978; Flores, 1982) suggest it was manufactured by the La Roqueta pottery in Palma. The main façade is capped by a spectacular, wavy mansard roof, with a scaly surface and roof ridges made from similar ceramic mouldings as the tan-coloured semi-cylindrical ones, surmounted by other pieces in shades of green and blue. According to the master plan these may be attributed to Sebastià Ribó. The part of the roof overlooking the rear courtyard is clad in ceramic *trencadís* with colours fading from brown to white.

Bulbous dome and cross surmounting the turret. →

Ceramic fragments covering the attic roof. →

TAXI
BUS

Attic roof. *Trencadís* detail between the tiles resembling scales on the main façade. ↑

↑ Attic roof. *Trencadís* detail on the back.

Climbing the residents' staircase, which is covered in white and blue tiles that take on different hues depending on the amount of light falling on them (they are darker when there is more light, and lighter when there is less), is an unforgettable experience. The blue tiles were made at the Ribó pottery, as can be seen by the name stamped on the back. The corners were decorated with fragments of the same tiles cut into regular shapes with a diamond tip. This means that the corners are semi-rounded instead of ridged. These are small details that may go unnoticed but reveal the painstaking care and attention to detail in the finishes.

← General view of the tiling in the central stairwell.

↑ Tile in relief on the wall of the central stairwell.

The rooftop is particularly worthy of attention. The washing lines were hidden from view in the attic, where the air flow could be controlled, and the clothes protected from the rain. The rooftop had a recreational purpose instead and was used by the residents from the block. The twin exit from the staircase, and the groups of chimneys are homogeneous in style, despite the fact that they served different purposes. They resemble long-stemmed, giant wild mushrooms: the chimneys, studded with glass and topped by cowls covered in glass and ceramics recreating highly stylised floral motifs, emerge from the same base. Some of the petals may have been made with tiles cut or scored with a diamond tip as they don't appear to have been cut at random and have very similar, repeated forms. We can also spot pieces of glass around the skylight that have been restored. They were always stuck to the cement ridged side down to ensure better adhesion, and the transparency of the glass made it possible to see the designs. Bayó remembers (Bassegoda, 2003) that glass balls coated with coloured sand or tinted cement, were originally placed on the top of the chimneys.

Details of the stylised flowers on the chimneys. →

Mushroom-shaped chimneys. →

The rooftop floor was originally covered with a special kind of *trencadís* (Bosch, Olona, 2017) consisting of pieces of the porcelain stoneware floor tiles from the flats in the original building, recycling the available materials, as Gaudí had done in his previous projects. The labourers cleaned off the cement on the reverse side and the tilers put them in place. The tiles were very hard and small — about 4 × 4 cm — so it wasn't feasible to break them into pieces. The porcelain stoneware floor tiles, especially if they had been manufactured by the Nolla pottery in Valencia, needed specialist mosaicists to lay them. The geometrical complexity of the design and the application of the tesserae, one by one, using the direct method, made the process even more complicated. However, at the Casa Batlló, Gaudí saved himself the cost of materials and specialist labour. Here, he didn't seek out the designs featured in catalogues, but new models stemming from the different approaches to laying the tiles shown by his workers, whom he no doubt considered capable of creating wonderful forms and designs without the aid of a guide. Bayó (Bassegoda, 2003) says that Gaudí told his labourers: "don't worry about the drawing, it will be what it will be", an extraordinary statement that we could extrapolate to the entire repertoire of *trencadís*.

↑ Main courtyard. Floor of Nolla tiles arranged in a free-form pattern, similar to the one that used to be on the roof.

The rear façade wasn't treated as a secondary wall as the owner could see it from the garden in the first floor flat. The mosaics continue the theme of the elements on the rooftop. The entire façade is an evocation of nature with highly stylised floral motifs that alternate with geometric shapes. It is also important to highlight the composition based on carefully executed symmetrical axes, resulting in a meticulous design, that was in no way anarchic and repeats the same patterns. It is a very different concept to the main façade where the coloured shards of glass and iridescent effects are the dominant elements. Gaudí planned an initial grouping of mosaics on the roof that forms a protective balustrade. The same design continues below and runs all the way along the top of the balcony outside the attic space. The balcony contains fourteen small circular openings with a triangle in the centre. Below these openings there is a magnificent floral frieze with a repeated motif of white flowers and petals. There are two mosaic strips running vertically on both sides of the façade that hang like garlands from the roof to the first floor. They consist of a series of different-sized circles containing flowers in rich colours and completely new shapes.

General view of the rear façade. ↑

↑ *Trencadís* mosaics on the rear façade evoking the plant kingdom with stylised flowers and abstract forms.

Following Gaudí's renovations, the outer courtyard on the first floor was a place to relax with a landscaped area that can be seen from the dining room. The floor has a central strip made of small pieces of porcelain stoneware that stretches from the back door to the rear of the courtyard, where there is a series of planters set into a parabolic arch made from *trencadís* and the same roundels used on the main façade. Old photographs show this strip was originally covered by a pergola or gazebo in the same parabola shape. Its purpose was to guarantee the owners' privacy and ensure they couldn't be seen by the other neighbours. There were Nolla tiles on both sides of the strip, which were arranged in a *trencadís* pattern at the four corners. The entire space was restored in the 1990s.

The Casa Batlló is laid out like a set of cells. The glass and ceramics on both façades, the pinnacles, as well as the tiles around the skylight, resemble a vast mosaic. We also find traces of fragments in the wavy glass on the staircase, or in the fire-gilded glass on the first floor. This leads us to assume that the image and form of the fragments and *trencadís* are the main elements of the building.

Courtyard on the first floor. Flooring designed with Nolla tiles. ↑

↑ Planter in the courtyard.

Casa Milà Segimon, La Pedrera
Form over colour

"The paraboloids, hyperboloids and spirals are rich in nuances, due to the constant influence of the light, making any ornamentation unnecessary"

Antoni Gaudí (according to Joan Bergós, *Gaudí, l'home i l'obra*, 1954)

Although colour plays an important role in Gaudí's architecture, the forms of geometry and his in-depth knowledge of this branch of mathematics led him to create an architecture that was always in motion and gave rise to extraordinary forms. The use of *trencadís* on the rooftop of La Pedrera, which marked a break from the colour palette Gaudí had experimented with previously, led to a new approach based on the use of a single colour that reinforced expressive meaning through sinuous lines and reliefs, creating forms which, when seen from a distance, look as if they have been sculpted rather than just clad in tiles.

La Pedrera stands on the corner of Passeig de Gràcia and Carrer Provença and consists of two apartment buildings built from scratch. The developers were Pere Milà i Camps and his wife, Roser Segimon, who was the widow of Josep Guardiola i Grau. Her late husband had left her a major fortune in his will and she invested most of this inheritance in this sumptuous building. Building work began in 1906 and was completed in 1912. It is a monumental edifice that broke with the municipal building guidelines of the day. The first thing you notice from the outside is the sheer power of the stone façade, which has earned it the nickname La Pedrera (the Catalan for 'quarry') but the building has many other wonderful surprises in store, such as the wrought ironwork, the mural paintings and the *trencadís* cladding.

Timeline:	1906-1912
Developers:	Roser Segimon de Milà and Pere Milà Camps
Location:	Passeig de Gràcia, 92. Barcelona
Type and use:	New residential building
Associates:	Josep Canaleta Cuadras (1875-1950), Josep M. Jujol Gibert (1879-1949), Domènec Sugrañes Gras (1878-1938)
Ceramics:	Tin-glazed white
Stone:	Stone from Ulldecona and other varieties from Sénia, Xert and Borriol; Macael, Tranco and Carrara marble (Asarta, 1998)
Green glass:	Early 20th-century bottles in everyday use
	UNESCO World Heritage Site (1984)

← B.Y.P. La Pedrera, postcard, de 1911.

In order to appreciate the *trencadís* elements we suggest two approaches: you can look at the building from the outside or take a closer look on the rooftop. From the street, our attention is drawn to the roof studded with brilliant white skylights that contrast with the sweeping cornice of smooth stone. These elements lend harmony to the building, creating a dynamic contrast between the materials used: ceramic and marble. On a lower floor, there is a narrow 'footpath' with galleries surmounted by small domes covered in white ceramic *trencadís* at each end. Their purpose is to highlight the undulating rhythm of the roof, framing the Latin inscriptions dedicated to the Virgin Mary carved in relief on the stone. In the original plans, there was going to be a sculptural group depicting Our Lady of the Rosary at the top of the central space, but it never materialised.

Top of the main façade. ↑

The rooftop contains a wide variety of elements made in *trencadís*, which are the result of experiments with this technique at the Palau Güell and Casa Batlló. They use a similar colour palette. The washing lines are hidden away in the attic, just as they are at the Casa Batlló, meaning that the project focused on the organisation and distribution of space. The six skylights are the most eye-catching elements. Four of them are clad in *trencadís* and the other two are rendered with cement, lime and plaster tinted in subtle ochre hues. The most recent studies by the building conservators conclude that, in the original plans, all the materials were to be covered with waterproof materials. However, in the end, they were only applied to the largest elements that could be seen from the street to keep building costs down.

↑ View of the rooftop.

The skylights are covered with different materials, including ceramic, marble and stone in different shades of white. The two that are most visible from the street were planned as independent structures. They are surmounted by crosses on all four sides. The visible sides of the skylights are concave and have curved shafts that spiral down to the base. The materials were applied in situ. The side of the crosses that can be seen from the street is covered in glazed ceramic while the side facing the roof is covered in fragments of stone and unpolished marble creating a surprising wealth of textures and contrasts. The remaining four skylights have the same shape, but two of them are clad in *trencadís* while the other two are not. Each one is surmounted by a cross. On one side the cross is cushion-shaped and on the other it consists of a circle divided into concave forms that create the actual cross shape. The four skylights were specially designed to drain off rainwater and, the ones covered in ceramic and stone, were self-cleaning.

A closer examination of the structure reaps rich rewards. If you take a closer look at the *trencadís* jigsaw puzzle you'll come across surprising marks and inscriptions, objects chosen at random — many of them with a history of their own —, fragments of stone from the façade, unpolished marble, pieces of pottery with different firing defects, glaze that has dribbled down the surface, overfired pieces, or pieces that have become dirty before being dipped in the glaze.

Staircase exits. ↑

On the rooftop you'll also come across the imposing groups of chimneys, which have been described in popular literature as "warriors". One of the groups, which stands furthest north, is covered in distinctive green glass made of fragments of bottles interspersed with the occasional splash of white ceramic. Gaudí had used glass to add a touch of colour in many of his previous projects, but with a difference: he had previously applied the glass flat onto the mortar, whereas in the case of the chimneys at the Casa Milà he had embedded the glass into the mortar, in a manner reminiscent of the shards of glass people would set into wall tops to prevent intruders entering their properties. This intervention has been attributed to Gaudí's collaboration with Josep M. Jujol (Josep M. Jujol junior, 1974), as it was executed at the same time as the ceiling soffits inside the hypostyle hall at Park Güell.

We can conclude, in all certainty, that La Pedrera reveals the potential of the entire spectrum of white: a colour that isn't a colour. Different materials, marble, stone and the complexities of obtaining a homogeneous white in ceramics, form the basis of this versatility. According to the ceramicist and restorer Manuel Diestre, white was one of the most difficult colours to achieve, due to the fact that ash and sand from the kiln often came into contact with the glaze during firing. When the tiles were tin-glazed, the firing produced different shades of white. This was the perfect technique for Gaudí who was so fond of chance occurrences.

The *trencadís* combines fragments of ceramic and stone. ↑

Shaft above staircase exit. ↑

↑ *Trencadís* made of bottle fragments covering a group of chimneys.

Church at the Colònia Güell
The importance of key materials

"The church has to bring together grandeur and need"

Antoni Gaudí (according to Eusebi Casanelles, *Nueva visión de Gaudí*, 1965)

Truth, beauty and religious splendour are achieved through spiritual quality rather than financial clout. And it was with this aim in mind that Gaudí designed a small church for an industrial model village and recycled all kinds of materials, some of them in very poor condition. He used them to create a mystical place of worship, as if every material, regardless of its purpose, or its state, could be transformed into something essential.

Timeline:	1908-1914
Developer:	Eusebi Güell i Bacigalupi
Location:	Colònia Güell. Santa Coloma de Cervelló
Type and use:	Church
Associates:	Francesc Berenguer Mestres (1866-1914), Josep Canaleta Cuadras (1875-1950), Joan Rubió Bellver (1870-1952) (in the town-planning project and the construction of other buildings)
Ceramics:	Josep Orriols, Barcelona; Ribalaiga, Barcelona; Terres i Mir, Barcelona; Vda. e Hijos de Juan Vila, Barcelona; Hijo de Jaime Pujol i Bausis, Esplugues de Llobregat
	UNESCO World Heritage Site (2005)

← Márgara. Colònia Güell, postcard, 1931.

Eusebi Güell had founded the Colònia Güell model village in Santa Coloma in 1890, when he moved his steam-powered textile mill, the Vapor Vell, from the district of Sants in Barcelona, with the aim of creating a place where people could socialise and live together in a more healthy environment. The factory, and the development — which had all the requisite buildings, decent housing, and also included a school and headmaster's house, a co-op, social club and theatre — were built by direct associates of Gaudí's, who gave his sole attention to the church. It took him ten years, from 1898 and 1908, to draw up the complex plans and, once building had commenced, he worked on the site until October 1914. Work continued until the church opened, unfinished, the following year. Gaudí abandoned the project, as well as the one at Park Güell, to devote himself entirely to the Sagrada Família. At the Colònia Güell, Gaudí envisaged a church with two naves, one placed over the other. However only the lower one was completed. It is referred to as a crypt, although we should point out that it isn't a crypt in the strict sense of the word, as this type of structure was always built underground in the foundations.

The church features different types of cladding. First of all, Gaudí selected a wide range of basic, good-quality building materials, like brick and locally quarried stone. The glass and ceramics include a surprisingly wide variety and large quantity of discarded materials, bricks, glazed ceramics that had been damaged during manufacture to such an extent that they could no longer be used for their intended purpose, and slag left over from smelting. He also collected material from his projects that were underway at the time. This is borne out by some of his notes kept in the Colònia Güell parish archive, which reveal materials were brought by cart from Park Güell to Santa Coloma (Galí, Lacuesta, Micaló, 2004).

Ceramic *trencadís* around the windows. ↑

↑ Detail of the *trencadís* around the windows.

The decorative elements of the church, covered in elaborate ceramic mosaics, are truly stunning and are the subject of a detailed study by experts from Barcelona Provincial Council (Galí, Lacuesta, Micaló, 2004). They contain easily identifiable religious symbols that emerge from the walls. They have been created using the small-panel technique and the indirect method described earlier in the book. In Gaudí's previous buildings, the mosaics were on an abstract theme. The floral motifs on the rear façade of the Casa Batlló are the only ones that bear any similarity in style to those at the church at the Colònia Güell. The church contains countless elements laden with symbolism, such as Alpha and Omega, or, in other words, the beginning and the end, and the staurogram, the representation of Christ on the cross. You can also see a large number of coloured fish, one of the most frequent symbols since the birth of Christianity, that appear to be swimming around the steep walls of the church.

Christian symbols: the fish, Alpha and Omega. ↑

↑ Christian symbols: the staurogram.

Trencadís at the church entrance. ↑

The most iconic element is the magnificent glass and ceramic mosaic in the tympanum above the door of the church, inside the monumental porch. It is provocatively modern and features Christian iconography next to motifs rooted in local culture. These symbols were studied while the church was being restored (Galí, Lacuesta, Micaló, 2004). The centre features an octagonal design, with the anagram of the Trinity, surrounded by other symbols. Although they are described in the work quoted above, we feel it necessary to mention some of the images, such as the torch symbolising faith and light; the plumb bob and the set square, symbols of builders and here interpreted as reason and justice; and the glass drinking vessel — the image of moderation — that represents temperance through an everyday, traditional object found in most Catalan homes. The mosaic also features a plethora of floral and plant motifs, such as the olive leaf as a symbol of peace, and the Jerusalem thorn (*Paliurus spina-christi*), which reminds us of the crown of thorns worn by Christ. Sometimes we have to use different criteria when making out the objects depicted.

↑ Details of the *trencadís* at the church entrance alluding to the cardinal virtues.

We must also mention the covering of the vaulted ceiling in the porch, with its beautiful hyperbolic paraboloids. The curving surfaces of the vaults at the entrance create rounded forms and are covered with unglazed terracotta tiles. The first surprising thing about them is the way the pieces used as cladding have been cut. They remind us of Gaudí's first interventions at the Güell gatehouses, not so much in the use of colour but because they are regular and symmetrical, like Moorish tiles. The fragments are made with unglazed flat bricks which were regularly used on flat roofs, as a roofing material for porches and to create the vaulted ceilings in traditional houses and farmhouses. Here Gaudí has had them cut into four triangles. The fragments of brick form a distinctive, ordered grid of great geometrical complexity creating different compositions (González, 2004). These unglazed fragments provide a contrasting background for the red and black glazed ceramic cross in the centre: the cross of Saint Andrew, which reminds us of the martyr crucified on an X-shaped cross that had arms of the same length.

↑ Portico at the entrance.

Detail of a cross inside the portico entrance. ↑

↑ The *trencadís* on the portico ceiling combines fragments of flat brick and ceramics to make the crosses.

The windows also feature a plethora of *trencadís* mosaics. They are framed by fragments of ceramic and glass with cross-shaped mosaics at the top, representing the staurogram. The mosaics around the windows protrude abruptly from the wall, framing the stained-glass windows in myriad colours. Once again, the personal imagination of each viewer can lead to different interpretations. Are they shaped like a flame? Or perhaps a tear that brings to mind a tragic accident suffered by a young labourer? Or pineapples, bearing in mind that the stained-glass windows look like pineapples sliced down the middle. Everyone can draw their own conclusions. Here we find the most traditional style of Gaudí's *trencadís*, but, in this case, each window was dealt with individually. He covered all the elements around the window, the intrados and sides, and even created a small canopy to protect the window when it was open. He used ceramics produced by a number of factories, but in this case, they were mainly sourced from the *Pujol i Bausis* pottery.

As far as the technique is concerned, Gaudí used the direct and indirect methods. The volumes were made using the indirect method by placing the fragments inside a mould. He mostly used coloured glass to create these pieces. The mosaics around the windows were made using the direct method and with a wide variety of ceramic materials. It is important to point out that Gaudí used many tiles in relief as well as tiles shaped like animals' scales on the roofs. They were often cut into four pieces to create the shape of a cross. He also interspersed his designs with pieces of 19th-century, 15 × 15 cm tiles. Studies carried out by Barcelona Provincial Council revealed that he also used tiles from the 17th-century castle, the Torre Salvana (Lacuesta, 2004), which stood at the entrance to the Colònia Güell. The seventeen windows were the subject of a special in-depth study due to the diversity of their designs.

Although the church is unfinished, it shows how the use of *trencadís* had evolved and made an innovative contribution to the project. We could refer to the presence of materials steeped in their own unique essence drawn from their history, which show us the value of durability. Gaudí tells us: "one should not seek out originality" (Bergós, 1954) and the Colònia Güell is a container of fortuitous elements produced by the industry or personal history of each one, which eventually become part of the constructive and decorative context, beyond the skin of the building itself. It is as if every material, whatever its shape, were both essential and the essence.

↑ Each element around the windows is different and covered in *trencadís*.

And, by way of conclusion, the Sagrada Família
(1883-1926)

"Beauty is the splendour of Truth; and splendour captivates everyone, that is why art is universal"

Antoni Gaudí (according to Marcià Codinachs, *Manuscritos, articulos, conversaciones y dibujos*, 1982)

Gaudí's masterpiece, the Sagrada Família, is a monument to his faith. His identification of the connection between truth and beauty formed the basis of his religious beliefs as an adult when he dedicated himself wholeheartedly to the Sagrada Família. The bell tower on the Nativity façade was the only part of the building Gaudí saw completed during his lifetime, but he had definite ideas about the colour scheme to be used throughout the church, as the model in his workshop showed. One of his last pupils, Cèsar Martinell, describes the meetings he had with the architect between 1915 and 1926, including visits from different groups. Surprisingly enough, he began these visits, on more than one occasion, in front of this model, to justify his argument that architecture should be multicoloured (Martinell, 1951). The model was made on a scale of 1:25, and exhibited in Paris in 1910, at the *Salon de la Société Nationale des Beaux-Arts*, as we mentioned at the beginning of the book. The model is now on display at the Sagrada Família museum having undergone thorough restoration. Jujol was entrusted with the task of bringing these colourful designs to life but, currently, the cypress tree above the door, with doves perching in its branches, is the only polychrome mosaic to have been completed. It remained unfinished at the time of Gaudí's death, as can be seen in photographs from the period.

Timeline:	1883-1926
Developer:	Associació Espiritual de Devots de Sant Josep
Location:	Plaça de Gaudí. Barcelona
Type and use:	Church of atonement
Associates:	Francesc Berenguer i Mestres (1866-1914), Josep M. Jujol i Gibert (1879-1949), Josep Francesc Ràfols i Fontanals (1889-1965), Cèsar Martinell i Brunet (1888-1973), Joan Bergós i Massó (1894-1974), Francesc Folguera i Grassi (1891-1960), Josep Canaleta i Cuadras (1875-1950), Joan Rubió i Bellver (1870-1952). After Gaudí's death: Domènec Sugrañes i Gras (1878-1938), Isidre Puig i Boada (1891-1987), Lluís Bonet i Garí (1893-1993)
	Nativity façade: UNESCO World Heritage Site (2005)

← Top of the San Bernabé tower in 1925.

Mosaics were only to be used on the tops of the spires, although we can find other coloured details, such as the cross underpinned by the cypress tree. Martinell describes a visit to Gaudí on 22nd January 1926, when the first bell tower had been completed. This encounter gives us an insight into how far building had progressed at the time (Martinell, 1951). Gaudí wanted to use the most expensive, and finest-quality mosaic made of Venetian glass that had to be ordered from Venice and resulted in a four-year delay in building. It was made with standard green glass, which is the most resistant, it was fired in a kiln and a sheet of gold leaf placed on top. The gold melts at a lower temperature, making it adhere to the surface of the glass. Martinell describes it in this way, although we know that to make gold leaf adhere to Venetian glass another layer of thinner glass has to be placed on top of the golden film to create a compact whole. The spires are dedicated to bishops and represent their insignias. They are in the shape of a crozier surmounted by a mitre with a cross inside it. The ring is represented by the gap at the base of each crosier.

Mosaic and *trencadís* were only used on the tops of the spires. ↑

At the base of the spire, beneath the bishops' emblems, we see letters made with white tesserae using the *opus tesselatum* technique, reading "Hosanna in excelsis". They are arranged vertically and are different sizes, getting bigger the further up they are placed. From top to bottom, they make up the words in Latin "Hosanna" and "Excelsis", separated by strips made using the *opus spicatum* technique that alternate pieces of brick with green and red ceramics. They were still not in place at the beginning of 1926, but they can be seen in photographs associated with Gaudí's death, such as the depiction of the Holy Trinity above the cypress tree, which features a Tau-shaped cross, also made after Gaudí's death.

We can conclude with some words of Gaudí's, quoted by Bergós, which reveal the architect's admiration for the beauty of a material that clarifies the meaning of the bell tower — to connect heaven and earth — and, at the same time, welcomes sailors who are approaching the city with its bright colours:

"Look at that spire! Isn't it true that it looks as if it's connecting heaven and earth? This burst of mosaic is the first thing sailors will see as they approach Barcelona. It will give them a radiant welcome" (Bergós, 1954).

Mosaic using *opus tesselatum* for the letters and *opus spicatum* for the vertical strips between them. ↑

↑ Depiction of the Holy Trinity above the cypress tree.

Many of the mosaic pieces covering the spires are made of Venetian glass, which is the most expensive and the best quality. ↑

Hosanna
Excelsis
Hosanna
Excelsis

The *trencadís* jigsaw puzzle
A covering to be preserved or discarded?

Jaume Coll Conesa
Director of the Museo Nacional de Cerámica y de las Artes Suntuarias González Martí

Since its beginnings, architecture has sought to make colour an integral part of its projects. Colour has been one of its fundamental and most visible components, to such an extent that its loss has led to the social and symbolic aspects of this synthesis of the arts being seriously undermined by people's negative perception of it.

Modernista trencadís performs a very similar function to tiles. It brings form and colour to unusual fragmented designs that we could consider the first repurposing of a ceramic material. *Trencadís* is a kind of collage technique that uses objects in a different way to their intended purpose (Duran, 2006). It isn't recycling, it is reuse with a new visual formulation.

Here are some of the key characteristics of *trencadís*:

— It represents a distinctive creativity espoused by a specific philosophy of architecture arising within a particular social and historic context.

— The idea behind it stems from a concept of authorship. Alexandre Cirici pointed this out when he said that the mosaic collage on the bench at Park Güell made it a pictorial as well as an architectural work (Duran, 2006). Its distinctive application, case by case, is associated with two creative agents: the architect and the mosaicist. The former designs and supervises the work, which is conceived as a whole whose constituent parts contain his vision for the project and the guidelines he proposes; the latter brings the creative details to fruition.

— As it is part of the complexity of an architectural structure, it has two key dependencies:

- One the one hand, it is an intentional element that reflects the expressiveness of the project and its identity.

- And on the other, it is an element that supports the former, its preservation being intrinsic to the surface it is being applied to.

The subsidiarity of *trencadís* to the architectural project was already highlighted by Antoni González, at the panel discussion at the Esplugues Congress, as a key part of planning a building. This is because it plays a role in the building as a historic document, as an architectural object and as a symbolic object of significance to society, to such an extent that it may be more important than the architecture that underpins it (panel discussion, 2006).

The innovative use of ceramic, and, consequently *trencadís*, has had to carry the burden that has accompanied applied ceramics since its beginnings: the need to use cement to help it adhere. The problems associated with the different ways materials respond, and the different criteria and possible procedures for preservation, were already dealt with at the preliminary session of the ICCROM and Spanish Academy meeting in Rome which looked at the study and conservation of decorative ceramics used in architecture (Almagro et al., 2001). The mechanical stability of the building itself also plays a role in the surfaces used as its may be affected by damp, movement, etc. In the case of the ceramic elements, together with the interdependency of the technical and building elements, their continued use is related to other factors, such as the structural stability of the material according to its physical characteristics: its nature, its durability, toughness, or porosity (Vendrell, 2003).

← Park Güell. Detail of the gatehouse roofs.

This first aspect is particularly important, as the ceramics applied may be made from materials that create a unity between the medium and its coloured coating, as is the case of porcelain stoneware, or may have several layers of a different type, as is the case with Majolica, which combines an underglaze fired with a second glaze. During the panel discussion at the Esplugues Congress, Antoni Cumella talked about what made some ceramics more suitable than others for use on exteriors (panel discussion, 2006).

Porcelain stoneware, porcelain, hard faience, or fritware, are less porous than terracotta and Majolica. The glazed surfaces obtained by fusing the glaze onto the ceramics, such as salt-glaze or feldspar-porcelain glazed ceramics, reveal no changes in behaviour when exposed to external physical phenomena. Nevertheless, when glass is applied to Majolica and china, the base and coating react in a non-uniform way making their conservation much more complicated. In this case, there may be a different physical response in the expansion of each of the surfaces, for instance, or problems in the adhesion of the base layer and the glaze that may have arisen during firing due to incorrect blends of pigments, underfirings or overfirings. The physical behaviour of porous ceramic materials with multiple layers is particularly susceptible to the problem of salts becoming trapped between the glaze and the ceramic surface. Salts have hygroscopic properties and this phenomenon can occur in environments where there is salty air, or where lichens, moss and other larger plant species are found. It can also result from mechanical alterations stemming from biological factors, such as termites', ants', insects' and birds' nests. The salts in the cement may dissolve in damp conditions and be transferred to the ceramic tiles and penetrate them if they are porous. When they come into contact with the glaze they reduce the adhesion between both surfaces leading them to separate. The cement can also crumble resulting in the glazed surface becoming detached from the tile.

Plaster cement was usually used for interiors, and lime and sand cement, or Portland cement, for exteriors. A mixture of cement made with unwashed sand or from salty environments is a source of problems. The use of non-angular aggregates can decrease adhesion. For its part, Portland cement had replaced natural cements since it was invented by J. Aspdin in 1828. It is one of the great enemies of conservation because it produces alkaline salts, including sodium sulphate. Another problem can arise in reinforced concrete, as calcium carbonate particles form in the cured mixture over time, meaning that the Ph levels grow from basic (Ph 12.5) to alkaline (Ph 8.5), resulting in the corrosion of the wire mesh and cracks in the supporting structures (Fiorentini and Fiorentini, 2001).

When conservation is compromised by the presence of defects, a clear diagnosis of the building must be made and the problems detected. This diagnosis must also list any problems found on the tiled surfaces and any damage that has occurred that may have an impact on their conservation, and make sure their causes are eradicated (Coll, 2001). However, the intervention criterion is the most problematic aspect. Antoni González and his team from Barcelona Provincial Council have carried out an in-depth experiment into the restoration of *modernista* architecture containing *trencadís* (González, 1993, 2006; González et al., 1994, 1995; Lacuesta, 1993, 2006).

We pointed out earlier that architecture viewed as a whole (structures, spaces and qualities provided by the countless elements of the different materials that underpin it), addresses the problem of the inability of non-structural components to meet the technical challenges of durability and permanence they are required to provide, as the role they play in the building is in many cases not just decorative but helps protect and complement the structure. Nevertheless, their inability to survive is accidental in most cases, and their alteration and replacement are factors that weren't taken into account by the architects who included them in their buildings. Their disappearance is due to the shortcomings inherent to the architecture, building defects, poor specifications of the materials provided by the technology of the day and, of course, the impact of people who have caused rather than solved the problems over the years. The conservator/restorer of the architectural landmark is confronted with a complex situation, as many of these elements are merely remnants and make it difficult to understand the work as a whole. Nevertheless, they do provide a highly important resource with a documentary value that helps us understand aspects from other times that are an intrinsic part of the building to be preserved.

Any conservation or restoration intervention involves administrative procedures that are, in some cases, complex and concern the levels of legal protection of the building. Not all buildings have protected heritage status, and those that do, find that, depending on their importance, this status doesn't always take the same aspects into account. They may come under a particular town planning protection order, which is usually divided into different levels (from smaller to larger: specific outstanding landmarks, façade and basic elements and, finally, full protection). These distinctions are made based on their status, either as an asset of local importance or an asset of cultural interest. Specific declarations, particularly in the case of more important buildings, require a master plan that will define the permitted interventions in the building. The master plan must set out the guidelines for the conservation interventions and establish the correct protocols to enable those in charge of the project to be able to put in place the necessary multidisciplinary supervision under the guidance of the competent authority.

There isn't a handbook of universal solutions to the restoration and conservation of buildings. There is, however, consensus that each case should be treated individually and each intervention governed by criteria agreed on by the multidisciplinary teams (Coll, 2003). We have compiled a corpus of the different restoration and conservation projects to help us see in perspective and evaluate the process behind these interventions and their outcome (Coll et al., 1995; Coll, 1996, 1998; Alva et al., 2003).

As we proposed at the ICCOM meeting in Rome, a multidisciplinary approach, which will set out the guidelines to be followed, is the only way to understand the meaning of the interventions in landmarks. Due to the sheer scale of the problem, we are unable to come up with a universal, across-the-board solution or formula. Nevertheless, in our view, a series of core principles must be taken into account when intervening to preserve our architectural heritage:

1. Principle of the unity of context. This is based on the practice of conservation in situ. In our view, this should be a fundamental, conditioning factor when considering and supervising the intervention, in order to guarantee that all the original materials in the building are preserved to the greatest extent possible, as they provide a valuable record of its history and heritage in their own right. Law 16/1985 governing Spanish Historic Heritage endorses this principle and considers that all the integral components of a building should be considered an immovable asset linked to its container.

2. Principle of safeguarding the moveable asset. When it proves impossible to preserve the original asset in situ, either due to the material nature of the object in question or because it is extemporaneous, and therefore a mere anecdote of its time, and not an inherent part of the heritage asset, this asset can be transformed into a moveable asset. This doesn't diminish its heritage value, as even when seen out of context with the relevant documentation, it is a heritage asset that is essential in order to understand the landmark. This is why we consider it essential to carry out the preventive conservation of the property at specialist institutions with the necessary skills, such as museums and museum collections, or on site using the right tools and competent specialists, following the guidelines set out in a master plan. The removal and appropriation of objects from the property constitute an act of vandalism that diminishes our understanding of the landmark.

3. Principle of "authenticity". The principle of authenticity is associated with the material nature of the asset in question. This material nature depends on the age of the asset, and the technology and knowledge available at the time it was produced. This is particularly noticeable in the case of ceramics as they have evolved as a material and brought assets of a different nature to each period. Moreover, authenticity affects the transfer capacity of the tactile, textural and chromatic visual values of each historic event. I understand that this authenticity must also meet the needs of our times, or, put another way, the conservation or restoration should be carried out according to UNESCO's recommendations and the different restoration charters that have concerned themselves with the problem of recognising what is original and what has been added, without relinquishing the solutions of the present that use the new materials provided by current technology. This is why finishing floors and claddings with hand-made elements, based on past designs, may be a mistake depending on the expected performance of the material. Preventive conservation has its own language, in which the preservation of the original element is key. Restoration has other connotations when it comes to restoring the original asset. Once the remnants of the past have been preserved, we have to perform an intervention that will ensure it survives in the future, deciding on the best technical solution necessary.

4. Principle of maintenance. This is the first criteria of preventive conservation that is essential to every project. This sphere of action involves the specific training of professional conservators and restorers of historic heritage assets as well as specialised architects, to ensure they remain watertight and are structurally stable. This is the only procedure that can ensure their continued existence.

As far as the specific problem of *trencadís* is concerned, below you will find some observations about possible interventions based on its condition, although, ultimately, it is up to the multidisciplinary team in charge of each intervention to decide on the solution to be adopted in every case.

— Weakness, disintegration or movement of the cement used to stick the ceramic pieces, creating the risk of them falling off. There are several possible forms of intervention. The best solution is to repair and reinforce the cement if possible. If this isn't feasible, the removal of the ceramic pieces should be considered with the cement still attached, bringing as many pieces away in once section as possible to preserve the original shape. After cleaning the mosaic thoroughly and piecing it back together, reapply the mosaic to the surface ensuring you use the right kind of cement.

— Loss of decorative surface elements. When a section of the mosaic has been lost as a result of pieces falling off, this is usually due to the reasons mentioned above, or defects in the materials used. In this case, we must work out whether enough pieces remain to allow us to reconstruct the mosaic and restore the original colours and finish. Instead of leaving blank spaces, it is considered better practice to fill them in with contemporary materials that will allow us to distinguish between what has been preserved and the new additions. This is to help people understand the original context and the preventive conservation intervention performed. I don't feel it is appropriate to use old materials for current restorations as this can create historically inaccurate, albeit well-intentioned, combinations. The use of original photographic documents from the period (if they exist) and the study of shapes, textures and colours are fundamental to getting as close as possible to the asset that has been lost, and in reconstructing the gaps.

— Disintegration of colours and changes in the decorative surface elements. In the case of surface erosion due to defects caused by salts or biological agents, resulting in a loss of colour and the glazed surface, the resulting element, although still partly original, must be considered missing based on the above criteria. It doesn't look as it did originally so keeping it in its original location would make it harder to understand the landmark. The element in question should be preserved but displayed away from its original location. It should be replaced by present-day materials that make it easier to distinguish between what has been preserved and what is new.

In any case, as many specialists have said on many occasions, there is no universal recipe. Each restoration must maintain the previous method and evaluation as a universal criterion that will serve as a basis to decide the solution to be adopted (González, 1993; 2003; Coll, 2003). There is a profusion of techniques and experiments in the conservation of ceramic materials in situ (Perla, 1990, 1993, 1995a, 1995b, 1996; Riu, 1989; Soberats, 1996; Ferrer Morales, 2007), even outside their original context (Coll et al., 2001; Rallo, 2001; Sanz, 2001; Torrijos, 2001; Carrascosa, 2006), but I believe we have to defend a fundamental idea: the best place to preserve an aesthetic heritage element is on its original site.

↑ Barcelona. Detail of the main façade of the Casa Batlló.

Epilogue
The splendour and decline of *trencadís*

The fragmented, colourful shapes of Gaudí's *trencadís*, have become an easily identifiable element that we immediately associate with Barcelona, particularly if they are combined with rounded edges. This should lead us to ask ourselves why *trencadís* — and, the dragon-cum-salamander at Park Güell in particular — have become iconic symbols of the city. Barcelona has a splendid past and a unique medieval heritage. Indeed, the main purpose of this book is to show that the *trencadís* technique, although based on earlier experiments, was not used on a regular basis until the 1880s. But how can we explain the fact that Gaudí and *trencadís* have become such a magnet for visitors, and for Barcelona locals too? This question isn't easy to answer, but there is one irrefutable fact: it is a beautiful mosaic technique. And there is a second, no less important one, the onomatopoeic sound of the word *trencadís*, which means 'breakable' or 'brittle' in Catalan.

Given our inability to understand most of the reasons for the popularity of *trencadís*, we should take a look at some of the new creations that, ultimately, are just a showcase for the changing tastes of the post-modern age. We are going to see pieces inspired by Gaudí's colours and fragmented designs, which have achieved innovative levels of creativity, together with merchandise that has flooded the shelves of the city's shops, from the most exclusive boutiques and select museum shops, to newsstands and souvenir outlets. You can even find items featuring *trencadís* motifs as the standard bearers of the Barcelona brand at airports, including T-shirts with the name of the city, soft toys dressed as footballers, and all kinds of trinkets, that give visitors a last opportunity to take an object that typifies the city home with them.

The ambiguous relationship between a work of art — the product of a specific place and time — and its subsequent interpretation under different cultural conditions, in another place and time, is a recurring theme in the artistic process. The distinctive, creative richness of Gaudí's *trencadís* has inspired many artists, architects and designers, who have taken the technique as a starting point for their creative endeavours, as part of a process that eschews the mere copy or interpretation. Joan Miró set the ball rolling in his collaboration with Josep Llorens i Artigas to create the wonderful tiled mural at Barcelona airport in 1970, following up a project both artists had undertaken at the UNESCO headquarters in Paris (1957-1958). Both mosaics used regular-shaped tiles, but in his sculpture *Woman and Bird* (1981-1982) — this time produced with Joan Gardy Artigas — which stands in Barcelona's Parc de l'Escorxador, the ceramic cladding of the artificial stone has the appearance of an impromptu *trencadís*.

However, the 1992 Olympic Games were the true catalyst in bringing colour to the city's public space, as we have mentioned before (Freixa, Saliné, 2016). Monumental sculptural ensembles and installations were placed around the city, among them Beverly Pepper's *Fallen Sky*, in the gardens of the Estació del Nord (1988-1992), with its tonal gradations of blue to white; Roy Lichtenstein and Diego Delgado Rajado's colourful *Barcelona Face* (1992); and the fountain, the *Font Castellana* (1992), where the ceramicist Madola (Maria Àngels Domingo Laplana) juxtaposes yellow and white ceramic tiles with the black and blue of other tiles.

↑ Barcelona. *Woman and Bird* (1982), Joan Miró and Joan Gardy.

↑ Barcelona. *Barcelona Face* (1992), Roy Lichtenstein.

Other wonderful examples of the use of *trencadís* are the roof of the Santa Caterina market (2005) where Enric Miralles and Benedetta Tagliabue worked with the ceramicist and engineer Toni Cumella Vendrell to create a vast mosaic; and the Auditorio de Tenerife (2003) and Palau de les Arts Reina Sofía (2005), in Valencia, both designed by Santiago Calatrava and clad in white *trencadís*. However, curiously enough, when it comes to the small-scale sculptures currently being produced, none of them directly reference Gaudí's *trencadís* designs.

We also find countless decorative designer objects, including tablecloths, ballpoint pens, pencils and stationery, T-shirts and fridge magnets, that provide small-scale mementos for tourists. These include Ann Swinnen's painted stones from the "Gaudí Collection", produced a number of years ago by the nuns at the convent of Sant Benet on Montserrat, textile designs and fine foods, such as the *trencadís* white chocolate bar by the famous Barcelona chocolatier Enric Rovira, the *trencadís* packaging used by the Barcelona chocolatier Cacao Sampaka, and the Nespresso capsule, which, according to its advertising copy, states that "our aim was to find an element that was representative of Barcelona and would become a brand icon at the same time". The exclusive gift items with their high-quality finishes produced by the ceramicists Serra are different in tone. You can also find household textiles, a brand of cava, and even the Scoopy Gaudí scooter; and in the field of graphic design, you'll find references to *trencadís* on ATO milk cartons, and boxes of Nestlé chocolates, as well as countless objects that have found their way into our everyday lives. At the same time, care must be taken to check the quality of the objects in terms of design and technique, because there's a fine line between the ironic and the ridiculous.

↑ Barcelona. Santa Caterina market (2005), Enric Miralles and Benedetta Tagliabue.

Barcelona. *Fallen Sky* (1992), Beverly Pepper. ↑

It is nonetheless true that most of the current output uses *trencadís* motifs to disguise its dubious artistic merit. This is the case with those construction firms that specialise in "recreating" the *trencadís* technique in projects of questionable taste, such as the dragon — a parody of the one in Park Güell — in the pond at the Parc d'Eliana in Valencia. Of course, most of the modern versions that fill the shelves of souvenir shops fall into the category of the vulgar or kitsch. The Gaudí mosaic bull is an example that immediately springs to mind. Costing 35 €, it has flooded most of the shops in the city centre. In addition to confusing two diametrically opposed cultural realities, it also overlooks the fact that Gaudí would probably been a staunch opponent of bullfights. The bull has other companions too: a *trencadís* female flamenco dancer and a pink pig with wings. You'll also find luxury items, such as the non-drip oil and vinegar cruets by Rafael Marquina — a modern Catalan design classic — with their glazed finish that imitates *trencadís*; and the list is endless.

Nevertheless, many of the above items, from a box of chocolates to a teacup, have something in common: they remind us of the salamander in Park Güell. More than a souvenir, they have become a metaphor for the city.

↑ Valencia. The shade house (2005), Santiago Calatrava.

↑ Barcelona. *Trencadís* souvenirs.

Gaudí
y el *trencadís* modernista

Presentación

En 2014, los pabellones Güell se incluyeron en el World Monuments Watch para llamar la atención sobre el singular diseño de Antoni Gaudí y las necesidades de conservación de los edificios. Esto condujo a una nueva visión del valor del modernismo de Gaudí en España y en el mundo y, lo que es más importante, conllevó una renovada apreciación del trencadís en la obra de Gaudí.

«Trencadís» es un término catalán que significa «roto» o «troceado» y se refiere a la técnica constructiva desarrollada por Antoni Gaudí para cubrir la superficie de sus creaciones arquitectónicas. El trencadís se extendió rápidamente hasta convertirse en la imagen icónica del modernismo, el movimiento artístico de finales del siglo XIX en España paralelo al Art Nouveau en Francia y Arts and Crafts en Reino Unido.

Se trata de una técnica que sigue dos ideas claves en la filosofía Gaudí: la representación de la naturaleza a través del color, y la economía en la construcción, hasta el punto de que el trencadís utilizaba objetos cerámicos «rotos» como principal materia prima. Como explica el texto, la técnica concebida por Gaudí consistía en romper objetos cerámicos para colocar, con sensibilidad artística, los fragmentos sobre las superficies. Para ello colaboró con el artista modernista Josep Maria Jujol, siguiendo la corriente en Europa de aplicar arte manufacturado a la arquitectura.

El uso del trencadís comenzó en los pabellones Güell, uno de los primeros edificios de Gaudí encargados por Eusebi Güell para poner a prueba a su imaginativo joven arquitecto. A partir de aquí, Güell le encargaría otros proyectos —Palau Güell, Park Güell, iglesia de la Colonia Güell— que serían reconocidos como Patrimonio de la Humanidad en 1984 los dos primeros, y en 2005 el último.

Cuando la organización World Monuments Fund se interesó por los pabellones, estaban cerrados al público y en mal estado de conservación. Subsiguientemente, el Ayuntamiento de Barcelona contactó con la Universidad de Barcelona, propietaria de los edificios, y firmó un acuerdo para restaurarlos a cambio de gestionar el programa de visitas.

Gracias al apoyo de American Express, World Monuments Fund desarrolló dos proyectos referentes a Barcelona y el modernismo en colaboración con la Universidad de Barcelona.

El primero tenía que ver con el Turismo Sostenible, un tema candente en la mayoría de los destinos turísticos. *Modernismo Invisible* es una aplicación de móvil que expande la visión del movimiento desde los siete edificios icónicos más visitados hasta un abanico más amplio que muestra la excepcional belleza de más de cien edificaciones de la época que parecen «invisibles» no solo para los turistas sino a menudo también para los propios residentes de la ciudad.

La segunda iniciativa es precisamente este libro, en el que Mireia Freixa y Marta Saliné explican la historia de Gaudí y el trencadís y su evolución en el uso de diversos materiales, desde lozas caseras recogidas de la basura hasta restos de botellas de cristal y azulejos, y documentan las técnicas tradicionales con el apoyo de la fotografía de Pere Vivas, que captura con gran belleza el arte del singular enfoque de Gaudí del diseño arquitectónico.

El compromiso de World Monuments Fund con la conservación del Patrimonio Cultural garantiza que un capítulo del libro estará dedicado a la preservación del trencadís. Los visitantes han criticado varios proyectos de restauración porque piensan que se ha perdido autenticidad al reemplazar fragmentos originales, pero degradados, por nuevos elementos cerámicos, a veces con una técnica distinta de la original. Para abordar este asunto, el libro incluye un artículo del doctor Jaume Coll i Conesa, director del Museo Nacional de Cerámica y Artes Suntuarias Gonzalez Martí, en Valencia, en referencia a la metodología utilizada en la restauración de esta técnica.

Las iniciativas de World Monuments Fund, y específicamente de World Monuments Watch, pretenden abrir un diálogo sobre el patrimonio, su importancia en nuestras vidas y el hecho de que con frecuencia estamos rodeados de enclaves que nos enriquecen pero no se aprecian hasta que se hace evidente su necesidad de conservación. Con nuestros muchos colaboradores y colegas esperamos que este libro dé pie a un diálogo semejante sobre la inventiva de Gaudí y el modo en que el trencadís enriquece las calles de Barcelona y deleita tanto a los que viven en la ciudad como a los que la visitan, así como a aquellos que puedan apreciar esta obra a través de la app *Modernismo Invisible* y este libro.

—

World Monuments Fund, fundada en 1965, está dedicada a la defensa y conservación del patrimonio cultural del mundo. A lo largo de la historia de la organización, se han realizado trabajos en más de 600 emplazamientos y más de 100 países. WMF ha tenido el privilegio de trabajar en España desde los años setenta y da las gracias a sus muchos colaboradores en todo el país. Puedes saber más sobre nuestro trabajo en www.wmf.org

WMF da las gracias a American Express por su apoyo a World Monuments Watch y a esta publicación. American Express es patrocinador fundador del World Monuments Watch. Para saber más sobre el compromiso social de American Express, visita https://about.americanexpress.com/corporate-responsibility

Introducción

El mosaico de trencadís cerámico es el icono más representativo de nuestro Modernismo y de la arquitectura de Antoni Gaudí i Cornet (1852-1926). Sin su aplicación no podríamos reconocer el banco del Park Güell, ni la fachada de la Casa Batlló, ni tampoco las chimeneas del Palau Güell o La Pedrera. Pero, ¿qué hay más allá de su manifiesta expresión y belleza? Es este un tema apasionante que intentaremos desbrozar en estas páginas.

Podemos ofrecer algunas respuestas que justifican el gran éxito de la técnica del trencadís durante el Modernismo. En primer lugar, la tradición local de recubrir los muros con azulejos de colores, un recurso higiénico y económico que se utilizaba en Cataluña y en Valencia desde la Edad Media, y que tuvo una gran difusión desde el siglo XVIII. Pero también tenemos que hacer referencia a la excelente sintonía entre arquitectos, diseñadores y empresas productoras que lograron diseños cerámicos de gran calidad que se producían masivamente para un público entusiasta. Lluís Domènech i Montaner (1850-1923) y Antoni Gaudí fueron los dos arquitectos modernistas catalanes que más a fondo exploraron las posibilidades ornamentales de la cerámica, del mosaico y también del trencadís. Pero fue Gaudí, con su colaborador Josep M. Jujol i Gibert (1879-1949), quien dio un paso adelante, llevando los recubrimientos murales a posibilidades nunca vistas. Con todo, otros arquitectos coetáneos también sobresalían en el uso del mosaico y del trencadís, como el también ayudante de Gaudí, Francesc Berenguer i Mestres (1866-1914), o Antoni M. Gallissà i Soqué (1861-1903), Josep Puig i Cadafalch (1867-1956), Alexandre Soler i March (1874 -1949) o Antoni de Falguera i Sivilla (1876-1947). Además, junto a los arquitectos que vieron las posibilidades plásticas de esta técnica, debemos tener presentes a los grandes talleres de producción como el de Mario Maragliano i Navone (1864-1944), Lluís Bru i Salelles (1868-1952) o Eliseu Querol i Vilarroya (1895-1980), por citar sólo los más destacados.

Este libro pretende hacer un recorrido por el uso que hizo Gaudí de la técnica del trencadís, aunque en los dos primeros capítulos explicaremos el contexto histórico y cultural del arquitecto para seguir con las diferentes técnicas del mosaico y del trencadís y su funcionalidad, así como la descripción de los diferentes materiales con los que se realizan. El capítulo tercero, el núcleo del libro, se dedica a analizar los sistemas de aplicación de la técnica en las obras de Gaudí, empezando por los pabellones de portería de la Finca Güell de Pedralbes, donde la cerámica se empieza a colocar según la técnica del alicatado hispanoárabe y, acto seguido, se *trenca* (se «rompe») para terminar recubriendo el exterior de la cúpula como si se tratara de una piel. Otros avances se encuentran en las chimeneas del Palau Güell, en la fachada y cubiertas de la Casa Batlló, donde experimenta, además, en la aplicación del vidrio, en la Torre Bellesguard o en la iglesia de la Colonia Güell, hasta llegar a los paneles de la sala hipóstila y el banco ondulado del Park Güell, donde, con la colaboración de Josep M. Jujol, Gaudí realiza una aportación plástica que preludia la estética de la modernidad. Finalmente, dedicaremos unos últimos capítulos a definir los problemas derivados de la restauración y conservación de los mosaicos de trencadís y analizar el uso y abuso que se hace de ellos actualmente.

El gran interrogante que ha planeado durante la redacción de este texto ha sido aclarar si fue Gaudí el primero en aplicar esta técnica. Creemos que se puede afirmar con rotundidad que Gaudí reinventará una práctica utilizada en el pasado e inventará una nueva fórmula moderna, ligada a la recuperación de piezas cerámicas en desuso. Pero la confirmación de la nueva práctica respecto a materiales y revestimientos nos la ha dado el propio Gaudí en una conversación de 22 de enero de 1926 con Cèsar Martinell, uno de sus colaboradores. Comentan la finalización de la primera torre de la Sagrada Familia, y Gaudí habla sobre el recubrimiento de mosaicos: «Los remates en punta que algunos arquitectos ponen en los edificios ...» (después de que él hubiera hecho la cumbre cónica del Palau Güell) « ...no tienen la vistosidad deseada debido a la poca calidad del revestimiento ...» (Martinell, 1951). Martinell justifica los remates en forma de pináculos como una de las grandes aportaciones arquitectónicas de Gaudí, pero reconoce también que su relevancia depende de los materiales. La cúpula del salón del Palau Güell que preside la azotea, y a la que se refieren maestro y discípulo, está elaborada con materiales de desuso, marés vitrificado de los hornos de cal, fragmentados y colocados sobre la cubierta con la apariencia de un trencadís. Esta frase pone de relieve que Gaudí, ya en su madurez, reconoce haber abierto una nueva fórmula en el uso del revestimiento de la arquitectura.

Antoni Gaudí i Cornet

El arquitecto del color

Antoni Gaudí cursó sus estudios primarios y secundarios en Reus, su ciudad natal, una localidad en pleno crecimiento con un proletariado en auge y una burguesía de carácter liberal. Más tarde (1870), la familia se trasladó a Barcelona, y Gaudí estudió en la recién creada Escuela Provincial de Arquitectura de Barcelona. A principios de los años ochenta del siglo XIX, Gaudí empezó a colaborar con el arquitecto Joan Martorell i Montells (1833-1906), quien ejercería una profunda influencia tanto sobre su obra como sobre la manera de entender la arquitectura. Gaudí siempre lo consideró su maestro. En los años anteriores a la Exposición Universal de Barcelona (1888), inicia el ejercicio de la profesión, y, como los otros arquitectos de su época, es fiel a un eclecticismo que podríamos denominar «premodernista», aunque siempre otorga un tratamiento especial al trabajo en ladrillo. En sus primeras obras —la Casa Vicens (1883-1885), los pabellones de acceso a la casa de verano de Eusebi Güell (1883-1887), o el Palau Güell (1886-1889), la residencia habitual del mecenas situada junto a La Rambla de Barcelona— el arquitecto debate el uso de estilos históricos, introduciendo, al mismo tiempo, propuestas de gran originalidad ornamental y constructiva. Poco a poco, va dejando de lado la recreación de diferentes estilos, para centrarse en una nueva búsqueda experimental tomando como punto de partida las formas y los principios constructivos del gótico y que podemos encontrar en el Colegio de Santa Teresa de Barcelona (1886), en el Palacio Episcopal de Astorga (1887-1894), y en la cripta y el ábside (1984-1900) de la que será su obra más emblemática: el Templo de la Sagrada Familia. Pero Gaudí evoluciona más allá del gótico cuando introduce el arco parabólico que es, al mismo tiempo, elemento sustentante y sostenido.

En los primeros años del siglo XX, Gaudí es un arquitecto apreciado entre la burguesía de Barcelona. Construye una serie de casas en el nuevo centro de la ciudad moderna, el Eixample, en las que se manifiestan las formas abstractas y orgánicas del Art Nouveau internacional, como en el caso de la Casa Calvet (1898-1900), mientras evoluciona hacia formas aún más libres en la Casa Batlló (1904-1907) y la Casa Milà, conocida popularmente como La Pedrera (1906-1912). Un caso de directa influencia británica lo encontramos en una de las obras más significativas de Gaudí, el Park Güell (1900-1914), en el que, siguiendo los deseos de su mecenas, proyecta una bella urbanización residencial para la alta burguesía. Finalmente, la iglesia de la Colonia Güell (1898-1915), la plantea como una especulación a pequeña escala de lo que debía ser la gran obra de la Sagrada Familia. Terminado el encargo para la Casa Milà, Gaudí trabajará solo para un cliente particular, Eusebi Güell, en los dos grandes proyectos que tenía en curso —el Park Güell y la iglesia de la Colònia Güell— hasta el otoño de 1914, cuando la familia Güell rescindió ambos encargos. A partir de ese momento y hasta la fecha de su muerte, el 10 de junio de 1926, trabajó únicamente en la construcción de la Sagrada Familia.

Desde muy joven, Gaudí mostró su interés por el recubrimiento con mosaico cerámico, como lo demostró en su escrito *Ornamentación* (1878), que comentaremos ampliamente en este trabajo y que citaremos a partir de la edición de Laura Mercader (Mercader, 2002), o a través de los textos recogidos por sus discípulos. Este interés le llevó a visitar, en 1887, con Montaner, los talleres de uno de los últimos artífices valencianos que conocían los secretos ancestrales de la técnica de la cerámica vidriada, el artesano de Manises, Joan Baptista Cassany i Folguera (¿-?). Este viaje está descrito, en 1903, por el propio Domènech en un texto con motivo de la muerte del arquitecto Antoni M. Gallissà (Casanova, 2002).

La cerámica, por su perdurabilidad, es la técnica idónea para aplicar el color a la arquitectura. El uso de la policromía era, como es sabido, uno de los grandes retos de los teóricos de la arquitectura del siglo XIX, desde Gottfried Semper (1803-1879) a John Ruskin (1821-1897) (Fanelli y Gargiani, 1999) y, lógicamente, también en los arquitectos barceloneses de la segunda mitad del siglo XIX. Elies Rogent i Amat (1821-1897), por ejemplo, director de la Escuela de Arquitectura de Barcelona en la época en que Gaudí era estudiante, convirtió el color en el elemento más destacable de la decoración del Paraninfo de la Universidad de Barcelona (1863-1892), el edificio público más representativo de la Barcelona del momento (Freixa, 2018).

Gaudí se formó en esta tradición colorista de la arquitectura que quiso llevar a sus últimas consecuencias. Si analizamos toda su producción, veremos que siempre jugó con el contraste de texturas y colores y tenía previsto aplicar estos principios en su gran obra, la Sagrada Familia. Había concebido la realización final de la fachada del Nacimiento totalmente policromada y así presentó una maqueta, en 1910, en el *Salon de la Société Nationale des Beaux-Arts* de París. Su discípulo, Cèsar Martinell, describe cómo Gaudí la mostró a unos alumnos de la Escuela de Arquitectura que visitaron el templo, el 23 de enero de 1915, diciendo: «el color es vida» (Martinell, 1951), una frase que por sí sola ya justificaría la redacción de este libro.

Las claves para entender el uso de la cerámica, el mosaico y el trencadís en Gaudí

Es imposible saber lo que realmente pensaba Gaudí, ya que fue un personaje de gran genialidad pero pocos escritos. Tampoco queremos aventurarnos a imaginar posibles ideas basadas en hipótesis personales porque el imaginario del arquitecto puede dar pie a infinitas interpretaciones. En cambio, vemos viable recoger los motivos que justificarían su interés por la producción musiva. En el escrito *Ornamentación*, pese a ser una obra de juventud, se pueden encontrar una serie de ideas que ayudan a entender los principios que lo motivaron a hacer un uso tan amplio de la cerámica, del mosaico y del trencadís.

La primera reflexión que queremos destacar trata sobre las posibilidades de economizar los costes de la arquitectura, una consideración que tanto se podría aplicar al trencadís cerámico como a la incrustación de piedra. Dice textualmente en este manuscrito: «La creación de la mayoría de las industrias modernas ha tenido como objeto la economía de la obra en los objetos fabricados. La adopción de la maquinaria ha hecho abaratar los objetos fabricados, pero ha puesto más cara la mano de obra. Este hecho se ha propagado por todos los ramos, y la construcción ha sufrido su influencia ... Pues si actualmente la mano de obra es cara y todavía es preciso suprimirla, sólo los procedimientos pueden economizarla, que lo demás sería una mutilación y no una economía. Todo se cifra en usar abundantemente lo que es de fácil adquisición y de suprimir o emplear escasamente las cosas de adquisición costosa» (Antoni Gaudí, transcrito por Mercader, 2002).

Por otra parte, es evidente que Gaudí utilizaba materiales de coste muy bajo para la realización de mosaicos. La industria de la cerámica representa una producción cercana y autóctona. Es, además, un tipo de industria que producía grandes excedentes de piezas —ya fuera por cocciones defectuosas, restos de almacén o sencillamente por estar pasadas de moda—, con buena calidad funcional por su impermeabilidad como revestimiento, pero más asequibles porque el acabado no era perfecto. Sin embargo, es necesario desmentir que solo utilizase piezas de desecho para la creación del trencadís ya que también utilizaba piezas cerámicas compradas o, incluso, elaboradas por encargo, como se puede apreciar en el banco del Park Güell o en la Casa Batlló, y también en facturas que aún se conservan. En otras ocasiones se parte de la utilización de objetos de reciclaje: platos, tazas o elementos de vidrio, como culos de botellas. Si bien este tipo de acabados normalmente se han atribuido a aplicaciones realizadas por Josep M. Jujol, es muy posible que fuera idea de Gaudí, como veremos más adelante, ya que la experimentación con estos materiales es anterior a la colaboración con Jujol.

En la cita anterior, también sugiere prescindir de mano de obra especializada, en este caso la de los mosaiquistas profesionales. Si bien la industrialización había fomentado la producción rápida, este tipo de trabajadores tenían un coste importante respecto de períodos anteriores. La técnica del trencadís evita los talleres especializados con la consiguiente reducción del presupuesto. Fragmentar la cerámica en teselas, pequeños cubos regulares, era un sistema demasiado caro para el revestimiento de muros de gran tamaño como los que realiza Gaudí en el Park Güell, la Casa Batlló o La Pedrera, y los pedazos del trencadís se producían con un solo golpe de martillo.

Otro concepto relevante es el considerar la belleza igual a la función, uno de los grandes principios de la arquitectura ecléctica: «Para que un objetivo sea altamente bello, es preciso que su forma no tenga nada de superfluo, sino lo que las condiciones que lo hacen útil, teniendo en cuenta el material de que se dispone y los usos que debe prestar, de los que nacerá su forma general» (Antoni Gaudí, transcrito por Mercader, 2002).

En esta misma línea, Cèsar Martinell, en la conferencia inaugural del Centre d'Estudis Gaudinistes, *Valor didáctico actual de la obra de Gaudí* (1958), definió a este como «un arquitecto de lógica estructural y de lógica decorativa». Esta lógica se recoge en el mosaico por tratarse de una aplicación con fines de revestimiento y de decoración.

Del mismo modo, Gaudí entiende que la belleza se encuentra en el color que surge simplemente de imitar las formas naturales: «La ornamentación ha sido, es y será coloreada, la naturaleza no nos presenta ningún objeto monótonamente uniforme. Todo en la vegetación, en la geología, topografía, en el reino animal, siempre el contraste de color es más o menos vivo, y de aquí que obligadamente debamos colorear en parte o en todo un miembro arquitectónico, coloración que tal vez desaparecerá, pero que la mano del tiempo se encargará de darle una propia y preciosa de antigüedad» (Antoni Gaudí, transcrito por Mercader, 2002).

La cerámica y el mosaico otorgan la posibilidad de dar color a la arquitectura y percibirla como un elemento vivo. Con el trencadís se conseguirán las variaciones de tonos deseadas que permiten la mímesis, es decir la imitación de la naturaleza. Si la realidad que nos rodea está formada por conjuntos pluricelulares que varían de color según el momento del día, la piel de mosaico o trencadís actúa como la misma naturaleza a partir de los pequeños pedazos que serían las células.

Junto con el color, la luz posibilita la percepción de los volúmenes. La refracción de la luz añade, además, una sensación de movimiento. Incluso cuando el color es menos apreciable, en horas tardías o en días poco radiantes, la luz es captada y proyectada nuevamente por reflexión, como si la cerámica vidriada actuara simulando fragmentos de espejo. Otra gran aportación es la creación de texturas debida al contraste entre materiales. Asimismo, la aplicación de la cerámica y el mosaico a la arquitectura tiene el valor añadido de poder percibirla a grandes distancias. En palabras de Gaudí a Joan Bergós, podemos recordar el ejemplo del gran escudo de trencadís que debía presidir el Primer Misterio de Gloria de Montserrat: «Encima del Misterio de Gloria tenía que ir un escudo de Cataluña de mosaico de 20 metros, que se hubiese distinguido perfectamente desde Monistrol» (Bassegoda, 1974).

Otras ventajas que Gaudí aprecia en el recubrimiento cerámico son de tipo mucho más práctico: la impermeabilización de los elementos revestidos, la perdurabilidad —sobre todo si la comparamos con un enlucido de fachada—, la pervivencia de los colores originales gracias a la resistencia frente a las humedades, y, también, por la autolimpieza, que se realiza, simplemente, con la lluvia. Para acabar, el mosaico y el trencadís aportan, a partir de los fragmentos, una gran flexibilidad para cubrir las formas curvas y redondeadas que tanto gustaban a Gaudí y los modernistas.

Más allá de las ideas defendidas en sus escritos o en las palabras recogidas por sus discípulos, el trencadís gaudiniano presenta una serie de características que lo hacen único. Podemos destacar, por ejemplo, el valor que da a los intersticios, los espacios que quedan entre las piezas. Para nuestro arquitecto no son espacios menores que haya que esconder y no es necesario ajustar con perfección las piezas para evitar que se vean. El espacio entre una y otra pieza puede mantener una distancia, incluso destacando sus bordes. En este sentido disentía claramente de los técnicos de los talleres, como Lluís Bru, para los que era imprescindible que las juntas se presentaran lo más cerca posible. Los nietos de Lluís Bru, Josep y Lluís, cuentan una anécdota muy conocida sobre un encuentro entre su abuelo y Gaudí, en la que el arquitecto decía que los fragmentos se debían aplicar «a puñados». En cuanto Gaudí salió del taller, el mosaiquista dijo a sus trabajadores: «No le hagáis ni caso, que él no sabe hacer mosaicos» (Saliné, 2015), en una clara crítica al sistema gaudiniano frente al método tradicional de los mosaiquistas.

No podemos hablar de la técnica del trencadís sin hacer referencia a Josep M. Jujol, un arquitecto muy relacionada con Gaudí y que también desarrolló una trayectoria muy rica y original al margen del maestro. Jujol terminó los estudios de arquitectura en 1906, cuando ya colaboraba con Gaudí, con quien había contactado por su origen común en el Camp de Tarragona. Se puede constatar su intervención en la Casa Batlló, La Pedrera y, sobre todo, en la sala hipóstila y el banco ondulado del Park Güell. A él se deben las intervenciones más osadas en el uso del trencadís, aunque siempre con la aquiescencia del maestro, ya que si analizamos la obra individual de Jujol, el mosaico nunca tiene un papel determinante o de recubrimiento masivo. En cambio, durante sus largos años de profesión, tocó registros muy diferentes, tanto en la arquitectura, con la búsqueda formal y técnica y la exploración de diversas tipologías, como en el ámbito del dibujo, la caligrafía y el diseño.

El mosaico y su hermano menor, el trencadís

El arte de los fragmentos para crear un todo indiviso

Las tipologías del mosaico en la Antigüedad

El mosaico se define como un sistema ornamental confeccionado a partir de pequeñas piezas yuxtapuestas. Visualmente se conforma como una superficie sobre la que se incrustan materiales como piedras, mármoles, vidrios o arcilla cocida de diferentes colores a partir de los cuales se puede desarrollar cualquier tipo de dibujo: geométrico, figurativo o abstracto.

La manera de colocar los materiales se resume con la palabra *opus*, que indica el sistema de obra o de fábrica, término empleado desde la época romana. La palabra *musivum*, mosaico, por su parte, nos remite también al mundo helenístico y al mundo romano. Pero, yendo aún más allá, encontramos la palabra griega μούσα que significa musa y que nos sumerge en la idea de belleza e inspiración. Se dice que los romanos recogieron esta palabra debido a que el arte del mosaico era tan sublime que sólo podía estar inspirado por las musas, lo que dio pie a hablar del *opus musivum* que significa «hecho por musas». Traducciones más estrictas y menos emotivas serían «obra de mosaico», «hecho de mosaico» u «obra mural».

Los primeros mosaicos, llamados *opus lithostrotum*, estaban realizados con pequeñas piedras, y su imagen será una de las más recuperadas por el Modernismo. El *opus sectile* creaba dibujos a partir de grandes formas regulares, generalmente de piedra y mármol, para generar formas concretas y manchas de colores, desarrollando imágenes geométricas pero también figurativas. Estos mosaicos nos recuerdan a los de tipo geométrico que desarrollará el mundo árabe. Poco a poco, el mosaico evolucionó hacia dibujos más perfectos y, como dejó escrito Plinio el Viejo, se desarrolló como un arte que imitaba la pintura, haciéndola perdurable. Según Plinio, en una definición que ha llegado hasta nuestros días, «el mosaico es una pintura realizada con piedra», un sistema perfecto para perpetuar la belleza. Este principio es el que llevó a crear los grandes talleres vaticanos, en la época del Renacimiento y del Barroco, que traducían al mosaico las obras de los grandes artistas.

La necesidad de perfección para imitar a las pinceladas de las pinturas obligó a cortar las piedras, los cristales y la cerámica en pequeñas piezas llamadas teselas. Si se observa esta unidad, por sí misma no tiene sentido; la pieza tiene identidad cuando forma parte del conjunto, el mosaico, cuando se percibe a distancia. Genéricamente se mencionan los mosaicos como *opus tessellatum* que significaría obra realizada con teselas, las pequeñas piezas cuadradas dispuestas en líneas verticales y horizontales. Pero la producción de mosaicos cada vez será más perfecta y esto condicionará otros tipos de colocación y formas de las teselas. En el *opus regulatum*, tienen el mismo tamaño, pero se alinean horizontalmente, no verticalmente. El *opus vermiculatum*, perfila el dibujo. El *opus musivum*, que ya hemos mencionado, es la aplicación que crea más movimiento, ritmo y belleza. Las teselas se ponen afuera siguiendo el contorno del motivo y ocupando todo el fondo. También es el mosaico que se utilizó como mural, pasando así del mosaico de pavimento al de revestimiento vertical. El diseño, la forma y el tamaño de las teselas o los materiales con los que están realizados los mosaicos serán fundamentales y crearán tendencia según la época de producción y las necesidades. El *opus segmentatum* nos recuerda mucho al desorden que produce la imagen del trencadís, mientras que el *opus spicatum*, que localizaremos en la Sagrada Familia es sumamente ordenado como la imagen de una espina de pez.

El mosaico y el trencadís en el Modernismo, color y forma para una nueva arquitectura

El arte del mosaico en el Modernismo catalán plantea una producción de una expresión única e incomparable respecto a las muestras musivas europeas que se desarrollan en el conjunto de estilos que engloba el llamado Art Nouveau. La recopilación de técnicas antiguas para generar nuevos mosaicos aplicables a la arquitectura moderna genera una gran diversidad de tipologías que tienen que describirse para entender la extraordinaria difusión que tuvo el mosaico en Cataluña. La nomenclatura moderna se tipifica a partir de los materiales empleados en el mosaico: piedra, mármol, vidrio o cerámica, y la podemos describir y definir a partir de la terminología aparecida en la publicidad comercial de los mosaiquistas de la época.

El mosaico romano era el producido a partir de teselas de materiales duros, como la piedra natural y el mármol, y servía, principalmente, para revestir pavimentos aprovechando la dureza del material y su resistencia a las pisadas. El mosaico veneciano, por su parte, se elaboraba a partir de pasta de vidrio coloreada importada de Italia. Había una gran diversidad de colores y calidades, y las producciones de mayor categoría eran las que reproducían colores metálicos, de oro y plata entre otros.

Finalmente, la tipología más representativa del Modernismo es el mosaico cerámico, del que deriva el trencadís, y que se impuso como el tipo de producción más habitual para la creación de los mosaicos modernistas. Realizado con azulejos esmaltados y utilizado como revestimiento vertical, al principio, en la publicidad, se le llamó mosaico árabe, pero acabó siendo tan popular que los mismos mosaiquistas abandonaron esta denominación para llamarlo genéricamente mosaico cerámico. Cabe señalar, sin embargo, que, en un primer momento, los mosaicos más comunes eran el romano para los pavimentos y el veneciano para el recubrimiento de muros, pero, finalmente, el mosaico cerámico se impuso sobre el veneciano porque la cerámica daba los mismos resultados que el vidrio italiano y su coste era mucho menor.

El trencadís, por su parte, se diferencia del mosaico cerámico por un factor eminentemente técnico, el método de corte de las piezas. Así, hablamos de mosaico cerámico cuando las teselas están cortadas con tamaños y formas regulares, una técnica que necesitaba de los conocimientos del mosaiquista para ser realizada. En cambio, el trabajo del trencadís, de corte irregular, no requería la destreza ni los conocimientos de un profesional, aunque también algunos talleres lo produjeron. Ahora bien, hay que aceptar que la frontera entre uno y otro es, a veces, complicada de determinar. Hay que reconocer que el trencadís, dentro del grupo de los mosaicos, fue considerado una técnica menor, por lo que esta denominación no aparece en la publicidad de la época.

Tampoco vemos representado en la publicidad del momento, el mosaico realizado a partir de piedras, el mosaico pétreo, el inicial *opus lithostrotum* clásico, que el Modernismo utilizó asiduamente a pesar de que nos han llegado pocos ejemplos. Eran aplicaciones producidas a partir de guijarros o piedras sin tallar, empleados en pavimentos o en revestimientos verticales. Gaudí utilizó esta técnica en muchas obras como revestimiento vertical, para obtener una imagen de arquitectura viva, en movimiento, incluso zoomórfica, auténticos animales vivos adaptados a su entorno natural y creados a partir de los materiales propios del entorno. La Torre Bellesguard, el Park Güell y la Colonia Güell serían ejemplos de este tipo de producción. La encontramos también decorando un techo interior de la Casa Roviralta (1903-1913) de Barcelona, también llamada El Frare Blanc, del arquitecto Joan Rubió i Bellver, o en la Casa Mauri (1905-1907), en la Pobla de Segur, donde fachada y jardín quedan decorados con este sistema. La voz popular recoge el testimonio oral de que se utilizaban guijarros del río, acarreados por las mujeres para obtener pequeños ingresos económicos.

La efervescencia del uso del mosaico provocó la mezcla de fórmulas de gran diversidad, creando lo que hemos llamado mosaico mixto (Saliné, 2015). Pero por encima de todas las técnicas empleadas, el mosaico cerámico fue el que se adaptó mejor a la nueva arquitectura modernista. El uso del trencadís ayudó mucho ya que se transformó en una herramienta de expresión única y permitió un ensayo continuo de modificaciones.

Las técnicas de producción del mosaico cerámico y del trencadís. Fragmento a fragmento

No se puede entender el mosaico cerámico si no hablamos de su producción y de las diferencias con el trencadís. Para realizar un mosaico cerámico, el primer paso consistía en pensar su ubicación. El lugar que ocuparía —pavimento o revestimiento vertical— definía la tipología del mosaico y sus materiales.

El segundo paso era producir las teselas, que se obtenían según el tipo de material. Los materiales más duros, mármoles y piedra, se fragmentaban con cortador, una máquina de volante manual que mordía el material cada vez que se hacía bajar la hoja. Para los materiales blandos utilizaban otros sistemas donde no existía ninguna maquinaria. El vidrio se empleaba, según los diferentes formatos originales de Italia, en forma de panes y también en pequeñas teselas de diferentes calidades en formato de 1,5 × 1 cm y grosor de 0,5 cm, que eran obtenidas a partir del corte con tenazas. La cerámica, por su parte, tenía una infinidad de sistemas para ser fragmentada y muchos mosaiquistas inventaron herramientas y sistemas personales para facilitar su corte. El método más lento era marcar con una punta de diamante la cara vidriada del azulejo y cortarlo a base de martillo y cincel, o con tenazas, y un pulido final de los bordes. El sistema más rápido, el que se empleaba en el trencadís, era la rotura al azar del azulejo a partir de un golpe de maceta por la parte no barnizada. Recogemos de nuevo la anécdota de los descendientes de Lluís Bru cuando Gaudí rompió un azulejo con la maceta y tiró los fragmentos encima del mostrador exclamando: «¡a puñados, tienen que ponerse a puñados, si no, no acabaremos nunca!».

Una vez obtenidas las piezas, existían dos maneras para crear el dibujo sobre el paramento. La técnica directa, el sistema utilizado en la antigüedad, consistía en insertar las teselas una a una sobre el mortero blando siguiendo el dibujo proyectado. Este sistema también fue usado a menudo en el Modernismo, principalmente en espacios rurales que copiaban la imagen del trencadís. Fue una fórmula muy utilizada por los técnicos de la construcción que sabían alicatar. Había que nivelar muy bien las piezas insertadas para evitar los cambios de nivel entre ellas. Finalmente, se esparcía una lechada entre los intersticios o juntas.

La técnica indirecta fue el sistema más habitual en Italia, empleada por los mosaiquistas en los grandes talleres vaticanos del Renacimiento y el Barroco. Las piezas se pegan sobre el dibujo en papel a escala real. Una vez secas, se cogía este papel lleno de teselas y se aplicaba sobre el paramento blando (haciendo una comparativa actual, sería como una hoja de piezas del moderno gresite). Cuando el mortero estaba seco, se mojaba el papel y aparecía el mosaico, y se rellenaban las juntas con una lechada. Este método ocasionaba algunos problemas cuando se hacía con cerámica, ya que la parte coloreada de la pieza era la que se enganchaba en el papel, por lo tanto la imagen final no se veía mientras se trabajaba, lo que podía provocar errores. Para evitarlo, se probó de trabajar con azulejos vidriados por ambas caras. Según se ha podido documentar en restauraciones actuales, Lluís Domènech i Montaner las utilizó en el Hospital de Sant Pau y en el Palau de la Música Catalana. El inventor de esta solución no sabemos quién fue. El Fons Taller Lluís Bru conserva azulejos vidriados por las dos caras de 15 × 15 cm. Los descendientes del mosaiquista, Josep y Lluís, atestiguan que un día, su abuelo, muy enfadado por un trabajo mal hecho, inventó esta solución. También tenemos una anécdota sobre estos azulejos relacionada con Gaudí. El arquitecto también fue a pedirlos a la fábrica La Esperanza, de Onda, de donde «lo sacaron a empujones», por lo inusual de la petición, según testimonio oral de Remedios Mundina, nieta de Francisco Muñoz, el amo de la fábrica. En realidad la parte barnizada tenía una pésima adherencia y era una mala solución a largo plazo, como han demostrado las restauraciones contemporáneas.

Otra fórmula que adquirió gran relevancia en el Modernismo fue la producción de mosaicos a partir de moldes para crear objetos con volumen, jarras, jardineras, etc. Gaudí aplicará este sistema usando medios moldes que se sobreponían a la arquitectura a partir del sistema indirecto. Se construía un molde de yeso sobre el que se colocaban las teselas por la cara no vista y se acababa de rellenar con mortero. Así se formaban paneles en relieve que, al girarlos, tenían la apariencia de azulejos. Este sistema es el que permitió a Gaudí —y a Jujol— la producción de conjuntos tan complejos como los del Park Güell.

La arquitectura modernista, y especialmente la obra de Gaudí, amante de las formas redondeadas, se dejó vestir con mosaicos. Estos, al ser producidos a partir de pequeños fragmentos, se podían adaptar fácilmente a esas formas. Remates de fachadas en forma de hastiales, cenefas sinuosas con relieve, o botones ondulantes conforman numerosos y bellos ejemplos de la arquitectura modernista.

En cuanto al trencadís, la misma palabra define la técnica. «Trencadís» (quebradizo, en catalán) es un adjetivo que significa «lo que se rompe con facilidad». Si bien la publicidad comercial, como se ha explicado antes, no recoge esta tipología de producción por considerarla menor, en cambio, las facturas de los mosaiquistas la describen claramente como trencadís o usan términos muy similares. El mosaiquista Lluís Bru la denomina mosaico de rotura o mosaico irregular, tal y como puede apreciarse en la documentación conservada en el archivo del Museo de Esplugues de Llobregat, dedicado a la cerámica de construcción.

En la técnica del trencadís se pueden apreciar una serie de pautas:

- Está hecha con materiales fáciles de fragmentar.
- La técnica de corte de las piezas parte del acto de romper los azulejos con descuido y como resultado tienen formas irregulares.
- El mosaico resultante da la imagen de un revestimiento fraccionado en trozos desiguales, colocados de manera que parece casual.

El punto principal que diferencia el trencadís del mosaico cerámico es que el corte de los fragmentos no es cuidadoso ni preciso. Esta aparente imperfección, precisamente, da a la arquitectura modernista catalana un aspecto de dinamismo y movimiento interesantísimo, único en el Art Nouveau internacional. Así pues, es a partir de las unidades o puntos de color (los fragmentos de cerámica) que surgen las formas y, en consecuencia, el diseño era espontáneo, a pesar de la indiscutible pauta de un modelo o idea previa. Los pedazos mal cortados facilitaban esta respuesta inmediata, de donde nace su principal característica: la gran expresividad y adaptabilidad derivada, precisamente de los propios fragmentos. Aunque este sistema de corte era rápido y la colocación también, la técnica de producción era eminentemente artesana ya que, en ningún caso, no se escapaba del corte manual ni de la colocación de las unidades de una manera metódica.

Otras técnicas industriales del Modernismo también llamadas mosaico

En la publicidad de la época, encontramos otros tipos de manufacturas para revestimiento que se anunciaban como mosaicos. La palabra mosaico, etimológicamente, implicaba una factura «pieza a pieza», y por esta razón, en muchas ocasiones, la cerámica, los hidráulicos o las baldosas de gres de formas geométricas se los definía acompañados del término mosaico. Pero creemos que también había otra intención. La palabra mosaico evocaba la imagen de la técnica clásica y la idea de calidad, belleza y riqueza, virtudes que toda decoración moderna tenía como meta indiscutible. Por esta razón se utilizaba muy a menudo el vocablo mosaico y se imitaba su imagen a partir de las nuevas producciones también industriales.

Los llamados mosaicos hidráulicos eran piezas especiales para pavimentos de interior realizadas en cemento. Los tamaños oscilaban entre los 15 × 15 cm o los 20 × 20 cm. Empezaron a producirse en Cataluña a finales del siglo XIX, y estaban realizados a partir de tres capas de cemento. La cara vista, era la única coloreada realizada con cemento portland, arena fina de mármol y pigmentos de colores. Para obtener las formas utilizaban trepas metálicas que separaban los colores y conformaban los dibujos. Se disponían en los suelos, como si estuvieran alfombrados, a base de dibujar un lienzo central rodeado por cenefas. Muchos de los modelos fueron diseñados por conocidos arquitectos y dibujantes del Modernismo. Existieron muchas fábricas: *Butsems & Fradera*, *Escofet-Tejera y Cª*, o *Orsola Solà y Cª* son algunas de las destacadas entre un gran número de productores gracias al éxito que tuvieron estos tipos de pavimentos. Gaudí también usó diferentes modelos en sus obras. La otra producción en cemento fue la pieza de relieve llamada loseta, realizada con una sola capa de cemento portland de unos 4 cm de espesor, que se utilizaba en los pavimentos exteriores. Reconocemos estas piezas en las aceras de las ciudades y también, durante el Modernismo, en las entradas de los carruajes y los almacenes. Gaudí, en 1907, diseñó el pavimento hexagonal que actualmente cubre las aceras del Passeig de Gràcia producido por la casa *Escofet*. Este elemento había sido diseñado para la Casa Batlló pero se aplicó posteriormente en La Pedrera por su complejidad (Griset, 2015).

Por otra parte, los mosaicos de gres se realizaban a partir de pequeñas piezas geométricas monocromas y creadas industrialmente. Eran de cerámica a partir de arcillas vitrificables a alta temperatura, y por su dureza se utilizaban en los pavimentos de interior. Las podemos diferenciar del hidráulico porque siempre tienen formas geométricas. Existieron varias empresas dedicadas a producirlas, las más representativas fueron la *Casa Nolla*, en Meliana, Valencia, y la fábrica *Llevat*, en Reus, Cataluña (Laumain, López, 2016). Gaudí reaprovechará este material en el patio del piso principal de la Casa Batlló. La fábrica *Hijo de Jaime Pujol y Bausis* también produjo este tipo de cerámica sin llegar a la popularidad de las dos anteriores, pero podemos destacar la aplicación de sus piezas por parte de Josep M. Jujol en la Casa Planells (1924) de Barcelona, donde encontramos un gran número de pavimentos con los correspondientes diseños preservados en el AMEL (Archivo del Museo de Esplugues de Llobregat). Sobre esta cerámica de gran dureza y que podía ser pisada sin problemas, hay que indicar que también se usó fragmentada en los pavimentos modernistas de tipo romano. Su cromatismo permitía crear diseños con colores vivos más allá de la piedra y el mármol.

Ambas técnicas manifestaban una intencionada voluntad de comparación, tanto cualitativa como decorativa, con el mosaico clásico —como la casa *J. Sas Villanueva*, con modelos que, como decía su publicidad, imitaban el mosaico romano—, y permitían una aplicación mucho más rápida por la fabricación industrial de las piezas.

También el trencadís fue imitado en cerámica, a través de trepas que dibujaban supuestos pedazos, recreando así la imagen de los fragmentos del trencadís.

A lo largo de todo el periodo modernista, fragmento y color es una reiteración.

Influencias en el origen del trencadís gaudiniano

Pero, ¿es el trencadís una técnica nueva? El interés modernista por el mosaico, seguramente se potenció gracias a los nacientes estudios arqueológicos locales y a la recuperación y el estudio de conjuntos históricos, por ejemplo los de Empúries y Centcelles, y los ubicados en los presbiterios medievales, como el de Santa Maria de Ripoll, restaurado por Josep Ubach hacia 1888 (Barral, 1971). Por otra parte, el mismo Josep Puig i Cadafalch remarcaba la valía de este patrimonio y la falta de estudios sobre las obras aún conservadas (Puig i Cadafalch, Falguera i Goday, 1909).

Cada una de las épocas en las que se desarrolló el mosaico en el pasado, Mesopotamia, Egipto, Grecia, Roma, Bizancio y el arte islámico hasta el periodo mudéjar, marcan influencias en el mosaico modernista. Este recogerá técnicas y materiales para transformarse en una producción totalmente renovada.

Debemos contemplar otra vez la herencia clásica que nos muestra producciones que se parecen a la imagen del trencadís. Hablamos de un tipo concreto, el *opus segmentatum*, que se utilizaba en pavimentos de tipo más funcional que no ornamental, elaborado a partir de piedras irregulares y de tamaños variados. La imagen sería muy parecida a los pavimentos actuales de terrazo.

De entre todas las épocas hay que destacar el conocimiento que tenían los modernistas, y en concreto Antoni Gaudí, sobre la técnica de los mosaicos hispanoárabes. La belleza de sus alicatados geométricos de cerámica sorprenderá a arquitectos e industriales que, utilizando una gran libertad de composición, llegarán a hitos insólitos hasta el punto de que podríamos hablar de una de-construcción de la antigua geometría de los alicatados.

Los orígenes más remotos los podemos situar en los alicatados que cubren los muros de los edificios árabes en territorio hispánico. Se trata de un revestimiento hecho a partir de pequeñas piezas de cerámica, regulares o irregulares, que se disponen en composiciones decorativas, obteniendo así un gran valor cromático. De la tradición hispanoárabe, se deriva la técnica mudéjar de incrustar pequeños fragmentos de cerámica en el mortero entre ladrillos, que da como resultado un recubrimiento de la arquitectura con contraste de texturas y colores. Luís Gueilburg, por su parte, cita también como posible precedente del trencadís, el *zillij* o *zelish*, utilizado en algunos países de la orilla sur del Mediterráneo y compuesto por pequeñas piezas de mayólica que los artesanos rompían entre las rodillas y enganchaban con mortero (Gueilburg, 2002).

Gaudí, como otros arquitectos de su generación formados en la tradición del eclecticismo, conocía perfectamente las técnicas de ornamentación mudéjares. Ya en las notas de su cuaderno de juventud, hace una relación de las láminas sobre la arquitectura árabe y mudéjar, según la colección de planchas fotográficas de las ediciones Laurent y Cia, que había consultado en la biblioteca de la Escuela de Arquitectura (Mercader, 2002). También debía conocer imágenes en color a través de libros de láminas hechas con cromolitografía, como el conocido libro de M. A. Racinet, *L'Ornement polychrome* (Racinet, s.d. làm. XXIX), documentado también en Barcelona.

Ahora bien, quizás el precedente más directo para Gaudí sean los paneles de piezas alicatadas que pudo observar en el pavimento del claustro del monasterio de Poblet, hechas hacia finales del siglo XIV, y que por aquel entonces todavía se conservaban *in situ* (González Martí, 1952). Por su mal estado fueron sustituidas por el actual pavimento, pero quedan algunas muestras originales en el mismo museo del monasterio, en el Museo Nacional de Cerámica de Valencia y en otras colecciones. Los paneles estaban inscritos sobre una base de baldosa de ladrillo y era obra de grupos de artesanos árabes que circulaban libremente y trabajaban por encargo (Altisench, 1974). La referencia escrita más antigua que tenemos de estos paneles, aunque la fecha de visita podría ser anterior, es del año 1915, hecha por Rodrigo Amador de los Ríos: «ciertos y muy curiosos recuadros de alicatados, que han perdido su coloración y el esmalte primitivo y que subsisten en el pavimento del claustro principal» (Amador, 1915). No aparecen citados, en cambio, en la visita que hicieron a Poblet los miembros de la Associació Catalanista d'Excursions Científiques, en noviembre de 1875, reseñada en su boletín, *L'Excursionista*; ni tampoco en la monografía sobre el monasterio de Lluís Domènech i Montaner, de 1915. Todas las biografías de Gaudí tratan sobre la fascinación que el arquitecto sentía por el entonces abandonado monasterio de Poblet. Gaudí lo podía haber visitado en sus años de estudiante gracias a la amistad que tenía con Josep Ribera i Sans (1852-1912), condiscípulo en la escuela de Reus y que acabaría siendo un prestigioso catedrático en Madrid. El padre de Ribera era maestro en un municipio vecino a Poblet, L'Espluga de Francolí.

Los primeros mosaicos modernistas. De Martorell a Gaudí

La técnica del mosaico romano utilizado como pavimento se introduce de nuevo en Cataluña a finales del siglo XIX de la mano de técnicos italianos (Voccoli, 2009), consecuencia lógica del desarrollo de la arquitectura neogótica en la construcción de templos. El fervor religioso decimonónico iba de la mano con la idealización del estilo gótico y la búsqueda de nuevos patrones para el arte litúrgico. El mobiliario, las vestiduras ceremoniales, las piezas de orfebrería, las vidrieras y, por supuesto, el mosaico, fueron el complemento idóneo. En la década de 1880, se empezaron a aplicar bellos pavimentos de mosaico en algunos templos de nueva construcción. El primer artífice italiano arraigado en Cataluña fue Luigi Pellerin (¿-?), que podemos documentar en la iglesia de las Salesas (1884), proyectada por Joan Martorell. Pero el gran maestro para los mosaiquistas catalanes fue Mario Maragliano Navone, que se había establecido en Barcelona en 1884, procedente de una saga de mosaiquistas de Génova, y que tuvo varios talleres abiertos en Barcelona y Madrid. En las postrimerías del siglo XIX, podemos citar a Josep Ubach (¿-?), con domicilio social en la calle de Les Corts Catalanes, y, ya entrado el siglo XX, al más conocido mosaiquista del Modernismo, Lluís Bru i Salelles, con taller en la calle Enric Granados a partir de 1904. Como muestra de la progresiva producción de mosaicos debemos hablar también de Eliseu Querol i Vilarroya, formado con Maragliano y Bru, con taller, desde 1914, en la calle del Dos de Mayo de Barcelona (Saliné, 2015).

Gaudí no participó directamente en el proyecto de las Salesas, pero debía de conocerlo muy bien ya que se realizó en una época en la que la relación con el arquitecto Joan Martorell era muy estrecha. También debemos mencionar el camarín de la Virgen de la basílica de Montserrat, construido, entre 1876 y 1887, por el arquitecto diocesano Francisco de Paula del Villar y Lozano (1928-1901) y su hijo, Francesc de Paula del Villar i Carmona (1860-1927). La decoración de dicho camarín, con la dignidad que requería el lugar, se completó con un bello mosaico, suponemos que realizado hacia 1885. Gaudí había trabajado en Montserrat como delineante en 1876 (Altés, Baraut, Galobart, 2013), antes de terminar sus estudios y, aunque en la década de los ochenta no mantenía contacto con los arquitectos Villar, seguramente conocía bien el proyecto.

En cambio, todos los autores coinciden en atribuir a Gaudí el diseño del pavimento en mosaico para la iglesia de las monjas de Jesús María (ahora convertida en parroquia de Sant Pacià), en el por entonces pueblo de Sant Andreu de Palomar y actualmente distrito de Barcelona. La realización, entre 1879 y 1881, de este pavimento se debe, según Bassegoda, a Luigi Pellerin (Bassegoda, 1989). La iglesia había sido construida por Joan Torras Guardiola (1827-1910), pero Gaudí fue el responsable de toda la decoración interior (Voccoli, 2009). Un segundo diseño de mosaico de Gaudí lo encontramos en el pavimento de la cripta de la Sagrada Familia (c. 1883), obra también de Luigi Pellerin, documentado en este caso por la revista religiosa *La Veu de Montserrat*, de día 29 de diciembre de 1888 (Barral, 1971), a pesar de que hay dudas de que el pavimento actual sea el mismo o sea el resultado de una restauración posterior a la Guerra Civil. En este caso, es probable que el nuevo pavimento lo realizara o restaurara Mario Maragliano. Ambos son proyectos de gran envergadura, a tono con la importancia de los encargos, y en los que se siguen los esquemas ornamentales practicados en los talleres de sus maestros, arquitectos de gusto ecléctico que justificaban la defensa del ornamento considerando que era el elemento que dotaba de carácter —y estilo— a la arquitectura.

Gaudí da un gran paso cuando aplica este tipo de pavimento a un edificio civil, la Casa Vicens (1883-1885). Quizá por el carácter privado del encargo, proyecta pavimentos de diseños y formas más simples que los de los edificios religiosos que hemos comentado pero que revisten el edificio de la misma categoría y dignidad. Recordaremos, además, que la Casa Vicens, junto con El Capricho de Comillas, con sus fachadas coloristas con piezas de cerámica aplicada son el preámbulo de la evolución que desarrollará a lo largo de los años en un proceso único para dotar de color a la arquitectura.

Antes de cerrar el capítulo, no podemos dejar de hacer referencia a las empresas de revestimientos cerámicos arraigadas en Cataluña, ya que la cerámica y el mosaico compartieron procesos de trabajo y producían la materia prima para la creación del trencadís. Los estudios de la cerámica antes de las restauraciones son la fuente de información más valiosa —muchas de las investigaciones han sido realizadas por la Diputación de Barcelona— para tener constancia de las empresas productoras. La empresa más documentada es la fábrica *Hijo de Jaime Pujol i Baucis*, de Esplugues de Llobregat, pero también podemos mencionar las fábricas *Sebastià Ribó* y *Josep Orriols Pons*, y las empresas distribuidoras *Ribalaiga Terrés i Mir*, o *Vda. e Hijos de Juan Vila*, todas ellas en la ciudad de Barcelona, por citar sólo aquellas de las que tenemos constancia — ya sea a través de catálogos, ya sea por el marcaje del reverso de las piezaas o por las facturas conservadas— que produjeron piezas aplicadas por Gaudí. Entre estas, tampoco podemos olvidar las empresas de Valencia, como *La Campana* (posteriormente *Peris*), *La Esperanza* o el gres *Nolla*, ni la producción balear de *La Roqueta*, en Palma, o las piezas de vajilla de porcelana de la fábrica *Pickman*, en Sevilla.

La evolución del trencadís en la obra de Gaudí

Paso a paso, obra a obra

De los Pabellones Güell a la Torre Bellesguard

Iniciamos un recorrido cronológico por las obras de Antoni Gaudí con el objetivo de analizar cómo va introduciendo gradualmente la cerámica fragmentada como elemento de identidad de su producción. Se localiza por primera vez en el recubrimiento del cupulino de las caballerizas y en las chimeneas de los Pabellones Güell de Les Corts. Allí inicia este tipo de revestimiento como si se tratara de una piel pluricelular, imitando los conjuntos de células que tiene la naturaleza. Un planteamiento mucho más maduro lo encontraremos en la azotea del Palau Güell de la calle Nou de la Rambla, Barcelona, que se construye casi en paralelo, con las populares chimeneas de trencadís cerámico, vidrio y ladrillo, y la cúpula recubierta con un mosaico de restos de piedra vitrificada, sobrantes de los hornos de cal. En último lugar, nos centraremos en la Torre Bellesguard, que se caracteriza por la utilización del mosaico de piedra, manteniendo el trencadís de cerámica y vidrio. Debemos considerar los tres conjuntos como unos espacios primigenios donde se fecunda un nuevo método del arte del mosaico, antes de convertirse en un elemento inseparable de la producción de Gaudí.

Los Pabellones Güell de Les Corts

La descomposición de la geometría regular

Cronología: 1884-1887

Promotor: Eusebi Güell i Bacigalupi

Localización: Avinguda de Pedralbes, 7. Barcelona

Tipología y uso: caballerizas, picadero y portería de la Torre Güell

«He cansado mucho a los que han trabajado conmigo, procurando siempre mejorar las cosas, pero no las he dado por buenas hasta que me he convencido de que ya no las podía perfeccionar»

Antoni Gaudí (según Joan Bergós, *Gaudí, l'home i l'obra*, 1954)

Esta cita de Gaudí nos ayuda a comprender que, con las primeras aplicaciones del trencadís cerámico, hacia mediados de la década de 1880, se empezaba a abrir un camino a seguir con constancia para alcanzar el gran objetivo de la «perfección», de la obra bien acabada.

De este conjunto, no queda ninguna documentación escrita, ni siquiera de tipo oficial ya que no se pidió al Ayuntamiento el permiso de obras pertinente. El primer biógrafo de Gaudí, Josep Francesc i Ràfols, que aún pudo ver los papeles del arquitecto en la Sagrada Familia poco después de su muerte, da la fecha de 1887 (Ràfols, 1928), pero la bibliografía posterior ha avanzado el inicio de las obras a 1884, fecha muy posible dada la complejidad del encargo.

La popular reja de hierro del dragón, el elemento más conocido y significativo de los Pabellones Güell, une dos pequeños edificios que tienen funciones muy diferentes. A la izquierda se sitúa la residencia del guarda de la finca, y en la derecha están las caballerizas, compuestas de un establo y un picadero. No era la única construcción que Gaudí hizo para Güell en la finca de Les Corts. Aún se conservan dos de los portales de entrada a la misma propiedad, situados, respectivamente, en la entrada de la Facultad de Farmacia y detrás de la Facultad de Biología. En estos casos, también se juega con el contraste entre el ladrillo y la cerámica vidriada pero no se recurre al trencadís. Construyó también dos miradores, ahora desaparecidos, que sólo conocemos por viejas fotografías. Uno de ellos se situaba sobre un inmueble no identificado —posiblemente sobre la misma masía reformada—, y el otro, adosado a un muro de la finca marcando un puente con un arco parabólico. Estas dos construcciones estaban decoradas con pequeñas piezas de cerámica incrustadas similares a las empleadas en los remates de los pabellones de la portería que comentaremos a continuación, pero no parece que se utilizara el trencadís.

La casa de veraneo de los Güell y su jardín

Joan Güell, el padre de Eusebi Güell, en 1859, había comprado una propiedad en Les Corts, Can Custó, y la renovó totalmente. Entre las reformas emprendidas por Eusebi tras heredar la finca, había el proyecto de trazar un nuevo acceso, abriendo una vía más rápida orientada a la nueva carretera de Sarrià, que se corresponde con la actual calle de Manuel Girona, y encargó a Gaudí la construcción del nuevo portal y de los pabellones de entrada. Se accedía a través de un camino privado, que cruzaba una serie de propiedades entre una doble hilera de árboles hasta llegar a la puerta del dragón. La entrada de la finca, en consecuencia, tenía un cierto carácter privado, escondido de la gente de la calle, un hecho que podría explicar el carácter insólito de estas construcciones.

La puerta del dragón y los jardines que lo rodean han sido interpretados como una imagen plástica del Jardín de las Hespérides, descrito en el poema *L'Atlàntida* de Jacint Verdaguer (Bassegoda, 1978). La relación de Verdaguer con los Güell se había establecido a través de Antonio López y López, marqués de Comillas, de quien había sido cura limosnero y que era el suegro de Eusebi Güell. Verdaguer terminó de escribir el poema en la masía de Les Corts que denominaba Torre Satalia, el nombre de una rosa silvestre (*Rosa moschata*). La primera edición de *L'Atlàntida* data de 1878, sólo cinco años antes de que Gaudí iniciara su intervención en la finca. Vale la pena insistir en la presencia de la leyenda de Hércules, ya que la encontramos también en el Palau Güell, edificio que comentaremos a continuación.

A la izquierda de la entrada, se sitúa la casa del portero, distribuida a partir de un espacio central octogonal —comedor y cocina a un tiempo— rematado con una cúpula de bóveda de ladrillos colocados por la parte plana (bóveda catalana) con un respiradero en la parte superior. A la derecha, las caballerizas están compuestas por dos módulos, el establo, de planta rectangular y cubierto con bóvedas de perfil curvado sobre arcos parabólicos, y un segundo espacio que hacía de picadero, con planta cuadrada bajo una cúpula hiperbólica con linterna superior. Desde el punto de vista constructivo, Gaudí emplea de manera magistral una antigua técnica de Cataluña, la bóveda catalana, que proyecta a partir de arriesgadas formas parabólicas e hiperbólicas. Pero también nos interesa constatar cómo, desde un punto de partida ecléctico, revisa los principios constructivos y ornamentales de la arquitectura mudéjar, muros de ladrillo con aplicaciones de cerámica, siempre a partir de una gran libertad de composición.

El exterior. Color, cerámica y trencadís

En los muros y las cubiertas exteriores, Gaudí propone un cambio de esquema ornamental respecto a sus obras anteriores, El Capricho (1883-1885), en Comillas, o la Casa Vicens (1883-1888), en Barcelona. Hasta entonces, Gaudí componía las fachadas de manera ordenada, como si fuera una retícula hecha a partir de la integración de azulejos sobre el paramento del muro. La ornamentación se obtenía a partir de esos mismos azulejos, hechos por encargo y con asuntos decorativos concretos, girasoles en relieve en El Capricho o claveles pintados con plantilla en la Casa Vicens. En los Pabellones Güell se rompe esta estética reglada con nuevos recursos —pone en práctica sus ideas sobre la arquitectura policroma mediante el contraste entre el ladrillo visto y el color de la cerámica, introduciendo, además, el trencadís— y empleando materiales de bajo coste o incluso recuperados. Observando esta evolución se puede pensar que se pasa de una arquitectura «engalanada» a una construcción de subsistencia con materiales muy sencillos.

Ahora bien, no todas las aplicaciones de color son cerámicas en este conjunto de edificios. En las fachadas principales, se encuentra un revestimiento de piezas de cemento prefabricado, teñido de un suave tono amarillo, sobre un zócalo de mampostería común reforzado con unas hiladas de ladrillo. En los muros interiores, hay rosas blancas y rojas —las rosas silvestres descritas por Verdaguer— estucadas dentro de unos círculos de fondo azulado, que se inscriben en círculos dentro de cuadrados grises o rojos, entre hiladas también de ladrillo.

En el remate de los muros del establo y la portería, hay una barandilla de ladrillo que dibuja unos triángulos equiláteros contrapuestos, en cuyos vértices se incrustan pequeñas piezas de cerámica que forman un punto central, por lo que la composición muestra un gran cromatismo y un orden que evoca la técnica decorativa y la geometría mudéjar. Están formadas por pequeñas piezas, cortadas con punta de diamante para realizar los cortes limpios, por lo que los bordes aparecen rectos y bien acabados.

En cambio, a ambos lados de la puerta del dragón —el pilar de ladrillo que hace de soporte de la gran reja y un pequeño portal para peatones—, ya podemos apreciar nuevos recursos en la aplicación de la cerámica fragmentada. Los intersticios entre ladrillos están coloreados de forma singular con pequeños trozos de cerámica insertada en el mortero blando con la técnica directa. El objetivo es dotar de color a la construcción, incluso al elemento más sencillo de todos, el mortero, material que se utiliza para unir los elementos constructivos y que aquí se convierte en material de adherencia para el trencadís.

Y aún se da un paso más en la decoración del cupulino del picadero y en las tres chimeneas de ventilación —y en menor grado del respiradero— del edificio de portería, donde el trencadís se utiliza ya de manera evidente. La cerámica es monocroma o con toques de color, en este último caso llamadas *fregalls* y jaspeados. Los tres tipos de cerámica fueron muy populares durante el siglo XIX, se producían de manera ingente en los talleres catalanes y tenían un coste menor que el de las pintadas con dibujos. Las monocromas, simplemente, se bañaban para obtener el color. Las de *fregall* (estropajo) —denominadas así porque se pintaban mojando estropajos de esparto en los pigmentos y aplicándolos sobre el azulejo— podían estar pintadas de diversas maneras y colores. Finalmente, los jaspeados imitaban los mármoles de categoría, de aquí las vetas que presentan elaboradas a partir de la mezcla de pigmentos muy aguados. Todos estos tipos de azulejos se realizaban en talleres que producían materiales muy populares, como revestimientos de zócalos, cocinas y espacios higiénicos. Los tamaños de estos azulejos eran de 13 × 13 cm o de 15 × 15 cm; más tarde se popularizó un nuevo tamaño, de 20 × 20 cm, según la aplicación del Sistema Métrico Decimal iniciado en los talleres valencianos. Es fácil pensar que el uso de estas piezas cerámicas podría ser consecuencia de la facilidad para obtenerlas más baratas debido al cambio de gustos y de tamaños.

El cupulino del picador presenta baldosas monocromas de diferentes verdes que recubren las jambas de las ventanillas de la linterna, mientras que en la cúpula dibujan triángulos que se decoran con un mosaico de formas rectangulares o triangulares. Las formas irregulares de medidas muy pequeñas actúan como fondo de color en los espacios libres, pero debemos pensar que siempre hay una forma geométrica regular y ordenada que domina el elemento. Por su parte, en las chimeneas de ventilación de la casa del portero, también las piezas rectangulares y triangulares, monocromas, de *fregall* o jaspeados, definen las formas y las piezas pequeñas llenan los vacíos.

Los Pabellones Güell marcan un cambio de orientación en la concepción del ornamento gaudiniano. Más allá del sistema constructivo árabe o mudéjar de incrustar en los muros y barandillas de remate piezas de cerámica, Gaudí, en las chimeneas de ventilación y el cupulino del picadero, añade una aportación brillante al reconvertirlas en *trencades* («rotas»), en trencadís.

El Palau Güell

La escultura funcional

Cronología: 1886-1889

Promotor: Eusebi Güell i Bacigalupi

Localización: Carrer Nou de la Rambla (anteriormente Conde del Asalto), 3-5. Barcelona

Tipología y uso: casa unifamiliar adosada, ampliación y reforma

Cerámica: Hijo de Jaime Pujol i Bausis, Esplugues de Llobregat; La Campana y La Esperanza, Onda; Pickman, Sevilla.

Declaración de Bien Cultural del Patrimonio Mundial de la UNESCO (1984)

«Todo el mundo se equivoca, pero el que menos se equivoca es el que repite sistemáticamente»

Antoni Gaudí (según Joan Bergós, *Gaudí, l'home i l'obra*, 1954)

El Palau Güell no manifiesta ningún tipo de elemento visible de trencadís a excepción de la azotea, un espacio totalmente secundario y al margen de los recorridos de la casa. Sólo se puede entender el edificio desde una concepción global, en la que construcción, decoración y creación de espacios se convierten en un todo unitario, pensado y cuidado desde todas las vertientes. Desde esta perspectiva, la azotea es un elemento también bello y lógico que culmina el proceso constructivo.

La construcción de un palacio

La idea de construir el palacio nace a partir del año 1884, cuando Eusebi Güell decide trasladar su domicilio en el Palau Fonollar, en la calle de la Portaferrissa, 9 —junto al Palau Moja, donde vivían los Comillas—, y compra una casa en la calle Nou de la Rambla, 3, contigua a la que había sido de su padre, en La Rambla. El proyecto uniría, de hecho, las dos viviendas (González, Lacuesta, 2013). La obra se inició en el verano de 1886 y se inauguró oficialmente con motivo de la Exposición Universal de 1888, aunque muchos elementos del mobiliario y de la decoración no estaban aún terminados.

Antes de continuar y entrar en materia sobre el revestimiento de trencadís, hay que hacer un inciso que afecta directamente a la producción cerámica en este edificio. Los estudios promovidos por la Diputación de Barcelona, actual titular del edificio, han demostrado que la decoración del interior del Palau se nutrió de elementos de la reforma que el arquitecto Camil Oliveras i Gensana (1840-1898) había hecho en el Palau Fonollar (Casamartina, 2017). Eusebi Güell decidió recuperar parte de los recursos decorativos de la antigua vivienda, entre los que se cuenta una parte del revestimiento cerámico. Esta manipulación de los elementos no representó ningún problema para Gaudí, al contrario, seguro que se lo planteó como un reto. Parte de las piezas aprovechadas se pueden ver en una fotografía antigua de la Sra. Güell en el Palau Fonollar con un fondo de arrimadero cerámico donde se pueden apreciar dos modelos de azulejo pintados con plantilla. Debemos deducir que se trataba de alguna zona noble del edificio, probablemente unos bajos, donde era común este tipo de revestimiento. Los materiales reciclados son un conjunto de azulejos con dibujo geométrico y floral que se repusieron en los cuartos de baño y en el lavamanos de la biblioteca de la nueva vivienda (Casamartina, 2017). Otras piezas quizás recuperadas, las encontramos en el techo de la entrada del Palau Güell, aunque no se puede descartar que fueran compradas de nuevo. Estas piezas están decoradas con motivos florales típicos de la producción del siglo XIX, pero con medidas de 20 × 20 cm —como acabamos de decir, la medida que se iba imponiendo por esas fechas— y todas pintadas con plantilla, símbolo de la evolución de la producción cerámica hacia la industrialización.

También formaban parte del Palau Fonollar los azulejos octogonales que se aprecian en la parte inferior del arrimador de la fotografía anteriormente comentada y que hoy podemos ver en la tribuna de la fachada posterior de la azotea. El modelo modifica su imagen inicial variando la colocación del cuadrado que rodea la pieza. Es muy interesante ver cómo, para adaptarse a la forma curva de la tribuna, se cortan los azulejos sin alterar el dibujo geométrico que forman. Con estos mismos azulejos también se decora la parte inferior de una ventana que da a la misma azotea, en este caso, enmarcados en un mosaico de trencadís de azulejos jaspeados en azul y otros blancos.

Un jardín de color y textura en la azotea

La utilización del trencadís más osada en todo el edificio se centra en la azotea, una zona que no era de paso, ni habitualmente accesible. Así que el trencadís de las chimeneas era una herramienta para colorear la fachada desde la calle, a pesar de que hay que hacer el esfuerzo de levantar la mirada hasta el remate del edificio ya que se trata de una vía muy estrecha. Superadas estas limitaciones, la visión es totalmente innovadora por el contraste de texturas y colores entre la fachada y las chimeneas, especialmente desde la esquina de La Rambla. Imágenes antiguas muestran, además, que en la fachada medianera había un impresionante mural al fresco, hoy desaparecido, de Aleix Clapés i Puig (1850-1920). El tema sería, según Lupercio Cruz (2015), Hércules buscando las Hespérides, con escenas o bien del canto primero, «El incendio de los Pirineos», o bien del quinto, «La Catarata», según González y Lacuesta (2013), aunque nos inclinamos por la segunda opción. Se trataría nuevamente de referencias a *L'Atlàntida* de Verdaguer, la misma temática que ya hemos visto en los Pabellones. Seguro que esta inmensa pintura llamaba la atención y conseguía que la vista siguiera el edificio verticalmente, detectando los elementos de forma y color de la azotea que surgen como verdaderas esculturas.

La azotea del Palau se reparte en tres niveles de alturas (González, Lacuesta, 2013), de los que sobresalen las chimeneas y la cúpula cónica como un clamor de color sobre la ciudad. Los niveles se mencionan como azotea de las criadas, donde se tendía la ropa, el de los señores, y el mirador, el más alto. La gran aguja que remata el salón interior, está situada en medio de la azotea de los señores y tiene múltiples funcionalidades: cubierta, ventilación, iluminación, pararrayos, veleta, y como no, belleza. El propio Gaudí, en conversaciones con Cèsar Martinell (1951), destacaba la importancia de este elemento que ofrecía nuevas posibilidades de recubrimiento de las superficies arquitectónicas, como se ha destacado en el prólogo de este libro. El otro gran centro de atención de la azotea son las veinte chimeneas, aunque algunas veces se cuentan dieciocho, ya que dos de ellas son idénticas y están ligadas por la base, lo que ha llevado, algunas veces, a contarlas como una sola unidad. De todos modos, hay que aclarar que, según el proyecto inicial presentado en el Ayuntamiento en 1886, sólo se habían previsto dieciocho chimeneas. Este hecho queda reforzado en los planos —copia de los de 1886— realizados en 1910 por Joan Alsina i Arús (1872-1911) y Joan Bordàs i Salellas (1888-1961) y presentados en el *Salon de la Société Nationale des Beaux-Arts* en París ese mismo año (González, Lacuesta, 2013). Debemos entender, pues, que dos de las chimeneas se construyeron posteriormente a los planos: entre 1889-1890. En su estado actual, todas mantienen la volumetría de época, pero el mal estado de los revestimientos ha hecho necesarias varias intervenciones, muchas importantes, pero todavía quedan algunos fragmentos auténticos de las piezas, fundamentales para estudiar las tipologías originales. Para conocer los elementos antes de su restauración es muy interesante la publicación realizada en 1990 (González, 1990), y para las restauraciones, principalmente la realizada en 1992, y sus criterios, diversas publicaciones posteriores entre las que destaca la del año 2013 (González, Lacuesta, 2013).

Podemos decir que una de las grandes virtudes de este espacio es el catálogo de materiales que utiliza, un manual nuevo de texturas a partir del cual Gaudí irá experimentando y que ya no abandonará. El primer material a destacar por su abundancia es el ladrillo, un elemento constructivo y no de revestimiento. ¿Qué similitud encontramos con el trencadís? La propia colocación de este ladrillo nos inspira la idea de «roto», como un fragmento geométrico y monocromo, que crea unidad visual con los otros elementos. Hay seis chimeneas construidas con ladrillo sin barnices, cinco ubicadas en la azotea de las criadas, y la sexta —una de las que no estaban dibujadas inicialmente—, en el mirador.

Las más significativas son las chimeneas revestidas de cerámica. Encontramos un importante repertorio de materiales de recuperación. Aunque se trata de fragmentos, puede apreciarse que, a diferencia de los Pabellones Güell, ya casi no encontramos azulejos de 15 × 15 cm sino de 20 × 20 cm, algunos aplicados directamente sin romper. Pero la mayoría de las chimeneas están recubiertas de trencadís de colores, las proyectadas inicialmente y que utilizan cerámica proveniente del Palau Fonollar. Por otra parte, debemos destacar una que está revestida de cerámica y porcelana blanca, tanto en la base como en la camisa y el sombrero. Se trata de uno de los modelos inexistentes en los planos iniciales, fechado hacia 1890 (González, Lacuesta, 2013), que se correspondería a la salida de humos de un hogar ubicado en la sala de estar junto al dormitorio de la señora Güell, una recuperación procedente también del Palau Fonollar. Es muy interesante ver el tratamiento del color monocromo y la utilización de tazas —cerámica de volumen— y platos de vajilla doméstica *Pickman*. En otra chimenea, el revestimiento son losas de mármol sin pulir que amplía esta idea de catálogo de materiales, elementos embrionarios que se desarrollarán en obras posteriores como La Pedrera.

Ampliando el catálogo al que nos referimos, encontramos, por primera vez, el vidrio como material de revestimiento. Se puede apreciar en tres de las cuatro chimeneas encaradas a la fachada principal que, hasta la restauración de 1992, aún conservaban fragmentos en la base y la camisa. La volumetría de estas tres chimeneas sigue el proyecto de Gaudí pero los cristales de los sombreros son nuevos.

Finalmente, queremos destacar una innovación más, el marés vitrificado que se puede apreciar en la aguja central y en una de las chimeneas —esta sobre una base de azulejo, principalmente blanco y sin fragmentar, que contrasta con la piedra de la camisa y el sombrero. Este último tipo de piedra procede de los desechos de materiales de los hornos de cal que Eusebi Güell tenía en su propiedad del Garraf. Son fragmentos de marés vitrificado que toman la apariencia de un mosaico pétreo. El marés utilizado para hacer cal se deshacía creando una capa vitrificada dentro de los hornos. Este vidriado ofrecía una impermeabilidad de gran calidad, ideal para la ubicación del cupulino sometido a todas las inclemencias del tiempo. Gaudí fragmentó este material y lo aplicó a pedazos sobre el mortero blando. Por otra parte, este acabado obtenido con materiales tan residuales ofrecía la imagen de un mosaico de piedra que también tiene su referente en la antigüedad romana. En la transición de los mosaicos de pavimento a los mosaicos murales, las villas romanas rurales adornaban las paredes de las grutas de los jardines con piedras —como la piedra pómez— y conchas de caracolas y otros animales marinos con una disposición similar a la que se hacía con las teselas (Buenacasa, 2006). No podemos evitar ver muchos paralelismos con la obra de Gaudí.

La distancia cronológica entre los Pabellones y el Palau Güell es muy corta pero presenta grandes diferencias de concepción de los revestimientos y, en el primer caso, los sistemas empleados son menos arriesgados y más antiguos. Por un lado, se utilizan azulejos más antiguos, de 15 × 15 cm, con diseños vinculados a la producción del siglo XIX y la fórmula de aplicación aún es cuidadosa y más geométrica, vigilando el corte. Pero la gran diferencia reside en que en los Pabellones la tradición mudéjar todavía está muy presente mientras que el Palau la mezcla de materiales y la originalidad de los diseños nos lleva a otro nivel de libertad creativa.

Torre Bellesguard

La piedra, revestimiento y recurso natural

Cronología: 1900-1909

Promotora: Maria Sagués, viuda de Figueras

Localización: Carrer de Bellesguard, 16. Barcelona

Tipología y uso: vivienda aislada, construida sobre restos del antiguo palacio del rey Martín I el Humano, restauración y nueva construcción

Colaboradores: Domènec Sugrañes i Gras (1878-1938)

«La originalidad consiste en el retorno al origen; así pues, original es aquello que vuelve a la simplicidad de las primeras soluciones»

Antoni Gaudí (según Joan Bassegoda, *Las conversaciones de Gaudí con Joan Bergós*, 1974)

La Torre Bellesguard (1900-1909) fue un encargo de María Sagués, viuda de Jaume Figueras, levantada sobre los restos del antiguo palacio del rey Martín I el Humano. Estos precedentes arqueológicos llevaron a Gaudí a introducir una importante carga simbólica y crear un edificio de estilo modernista pero con fuertes reminiscencias medievalizantes. Los pocos restos arqueológicos que quedaban del palacio dejaron trabajar de una manera totalmente libre al arquitecto.

Una de las principales herramientas constructivas y decorativas en Bellesguard es la piedra. De esta manera, los materiales originales y los procesos constructivos primigenios son las herramientas fundamentales para construir y ornamentar esta obra. En Bellesguard, sin embargo, no son desechos de producción como en el caso de la aguja del Palau Güell, sino que provienen de los materiales existentes en el entorno, en sintonía con las nociones de economía y de integración tan valoradas por el arquitecto. Se trata de una piedra delgada de una veta de pizarra, propia de la parte baja de la sierra de Collserola (Vall, 2014), que produce unos tornasolados de gran riqueza. Así pues, el material original ayuda a integrar el edificio en el entorno natural a través de los matices cromáticos y su textura.

Sin embargo, hay que señalar un breve precedente donde Gaudí aplica la piedra natural por primera vez, aunque no se relaciona con el entorno natural. Nos referimos a los escudos de la fachada de las Teresianas de Barcelona (1888-1890) donde nos muestra una base de piedras sobre las que se aplican los símbolos religiosos en cerámica de relieve. La piedra de Bellesguard, en cambio, se utilizará como elemento constructivo y decorativo a la vez en todas las fachadas, en un tipo de técnica que, sin ser un mosaico, acaba teniendo la misma función ornamental. Por otra parte, una de las grandes aportaciones en los sistemas de aplicación será la utilización de los medios moldes que ya hemos explicado anteriormente, lo que permite crear composiciones en relieve, en este caso con piedras como material básico. De este modo, puede modelar formas diferentes que ofrecen la imagen de un acabado en almohadillado. Tanto la puerta principal como todas las ventanas presentan una especie de marco a modo de gran moldura.

En el sitio más importante y visible de la construcción, la aguja de la torre de 33 metros de altura, Gaudí utiliza el trencadís de cerámica y vidrio. Se inicia con un mosaico de trencadís de vidrio con las cuatro barras de la bandera catalana, que ascienden helicoidalmente, hasta llegar a un módulo en forma de corona real que, a su vez, es la base de la cruz que señala los cuatro puntos cardinales. Así, esta técnica del trencadís adquiere una nueva relevancia; abandona las azoteas para situarse en el lugar más importante con la intención de que se vea desde gran distancia. Los fragmentos de vidrio están aplicados con el sistema de técnica directa y el color se había pintado previamente sobre los cristales transparentes en el lado adherido al mortero, la bandera en amarillos y rojos, la corona en blanco, y la cruz también en blanco con rojo en las puntas de los cuatro brazos. En la restauración de 1984, realizada por Bassegoda (1930 a 2012), aún se podían ver restos de los colores iniciales sobre el mortero a pesar de la pérdida casi total de los trozos de vidrio. En la base, un escudo de Cataluña en piedra muestra la fecha de finalización de la torre (1909), indicando que, a pesar de haber sido destruida en dos ocasiones, en 1652 y en 1714, es levantada de nuevo y nunca más volverá a ser derruida (Vall, 2014).

Otro elemento de mosaico a tener en cuenta es el pequeño panel que preside la puerta de acceso de la entrada dentro de uno de los almohadillados de piedras y donde puede leerse «Bell Esguard» (Bella Vista). Es un panel de pequeñas dimensiones, de cristal veneciano y de gran calidad de acabados, creado sin lugar a dudas en un taller de mosaiquista.

La otra aplicación que podemos atribuir a Gaudí es el mosaico de pavimento que preside la entrada. Por su funcionalidad, probablemente es original y recuerda la aplicación de mosaicos de tipo portugués realizada con grandes fragmentos de piedra geométrica, aquí, evidentemente utilizando las piedras del lugar y creando unos dibujos geométricos muy sencillos.

El entorno del edificio está totalmente amueblado con bancos y elementos de jardín en mosaico de cerámica de teselas y trencadís. Esta producción está dirigida y proyectada por el arquitecto Domènec Sugrañes i Gras (1878-1938), colaborador de Gaudí en varias obras. Gaudí deja de trabajar en Bellesguard en 1909, pero hay unos años de trabajo en común y Sugrañes continuó trabajando hasta 1917 (Subias, 2014). Los bancos cerámicos más antiguos se pueden datar, a partir de fotografías, entre 1902 y 1904 (Subias, 2014).

En la Torre Bellesguard, empezamos a ver diferentes muestras de procesos y aplicaciones que ya han roto con toda la estética anterior. Podemos encontrar la utilización de piedra del mismo emplazamiento, la creación de almohadillados de mosaico o trencadís elaborados a partir de moldes, el uso del vidrio como principal material del elemento más significativo de la fachada y, finalmente, la aparición de formas curvas, en sintonía con el cambio de gusto estético del Art Nouveau. Pero lo más destacado es ver cómo un revestimiento elaborado a base de fragmentos abarca toda la construcción, y de esta manera, junto con las formas redondeadas, despiertan la visión de obra total y en movimiento. Podemos interpretar el conjunto del monumento como una gran estatua de tamaño monumental que, vista desde el exterior, adquiere además una perspectiva amplificada gracias a la disposición del viaducto, diseñado por el mismo Gaudí como una proyección del muro.

Del Park Güell a la Sagrada Familia

Planteamos ahora el análisis de un conjunto de obras que se realizan paralelamente entre 1900 y 1914, y que tendrá un punto final muy tardío, en 1926, en la Sagrada Familia. Una parte importante del capítulo se dedica al Park Güell, un conjunto monumental que por sí solo es un catálogo de los sistemas de aplicación de revestimientos de Gaudí a lo largo de toda su producción. En él, podemos apreciar tres etapas y tres sistemas muy diferentes en la aplicación del trencadís. Un primer momento, antes de 1903, en las cubiertas de los dos pabellones de la entrada principal, en los paramentos y almenas de la escalinata, en el muro de cierre del Park y también en la construcción de los viaductos. Una segunda etapa, en la realización de los paneles de la sala hipóstila, entre 1907 y 1909. Y, por último, el gran banco ondulado hasta 1914. Desde 1907, fue fundamental la labor realizada por Josep M. Jujol, el gran artífice de estas extraordinarias creaciones.

Al mismo tiempo, Gaudí proyecta la Casa Batlló (1904-1906), en la que el trencadís envuelve toda la construcción como una filigrana en la que confluyen diferentes técnicas, texturas y colores; y La Pedrera (1906-1911), basada en el uso de un solo color, rompiendo los cromatismos experimentados anteriormente. Toda su experiencia culmina en los revestimientos de la iglesia de la Colonia Güell, una obra de muy larga gestación (desde 1898 hasta 1915).

En otoño de 1914, Gaudí abandona los encargos con los Güell y se dedica sólo a la obra de la Sagrada Familia. La única torre que vio acabada, la de San Bernabé, que tiene un hermoso acabado de trencadís de cerámica y vidrio, es una última muestra de la confianza que el arquitecto tuvo siempre en este tipo de recubrimiento.

Gaudí acerca su arquitectura a la naturaleza creando conjuntos que se integran en ella como un elemento más. Para conseguirlo, la arquitectura copia la naturaleza y la transforma en una verdadera obra de arte de medidas gigantescas donde el trencadís es uno de los principales sistemas para llevarlo a cabo.

El Park Güell

Cerámica y vidrio, el color en la Muntanya Pelada

Cronología: 1900-1914

Promotor: Eusebi Güell i Bacigalupi

Localización: Carrer d'Olot. Barcelona

Tipología y uso: urbanización residencial y parque

Colaboradores: Josep M. Jujol, Joan Rubió i Bellver, Francesc Berenguer

Cerámica: Fábrica Peris, Onda (cerámica pintada con plantilla y cerámica monocroma); Fábrica Hijo de Jaime Pujol i Bausis, Esplugues de Llobregat (cerámica pintada con plantilla, cerámica monocroma y piezas en relieve); fábrica Sebastià Ribó, Barcelona (los discos de cuatro medidas diferentes que se aplicarán posteriormente en la Casa Batlló); Pickman, Sevilla (vajilla de porcelana)

Vidrio: Tallers Pelegrí (según testimonio del constructor Josep Bayó)

Declaración de Bien Cultural del Patrimoni Mundial de la UNESCO (1984)

«Indudablemente, la distancia a la que se ha de ver un objeto implica un modo de composición adecuado al caso»

(Transcrito por Laura Mercader, «La distancia y el punto de vista», en *Antoni Gaudí, escritos y documentos*, 2002)

El Park Güell es la obra más ambiciosa de Gaudí en su trayectoria ascendente para integrar la cerámica —y el trencadís— en la arquitectura. Se trata de un desmesurado proyecto de intervención en la naturaleza en el que, de manera continuada, se rompen los límites entre el acto creativo del artista-arquitecto y la potencia de la naturaleza. No debe olvidarse que el diálogo del arte con la naturaleza ha sido una de las grandes cuestiones a lo largo de la historia de la creación artística, un diálogo que Gaudí resuelve de manera dramática y excepcional a base de incrementar la tensión entre estos dos principios.

El Park Güell, una urbanización para familias acomodadas

Eusebi Güell, el 29 de julio de 1899, adquirió la propiedad de Can Muntaner de Dalt a Salvador de Samà de Torrents, Marqués de Marianao, quien, a su vez, lo había hecho a la familia Larrard el año anterior. El objetivo era construir una urbanización siguiendo los sistemas británicos de casas rodeadas de jardín; de ahí que lo denominara Park, con «k». Muy poco después, en octubre de 1900, se comenzaron las obras de explanación; en enero de 1903 estaban terminados los viaductos y calles, el cierre de la finca, los dos pabellones de la entrada principal y la escalinata presidida por el dragón; y hecha una parte de la gran explanada. En 1906 se empezó a levantar la sala hipóstila, y el mes de marzo de 1909 se inició la construcción del banco cerámico que rodea la gran plaza. Pero en 1914, se paralizaron las obras cuando el primitivo proyecto de urbanización se dio por fracasado. No se construyeron más viviendas, aunque la obra del parque ya estaba terminada excepto la construcción de una capilla, que se desestimó, en la cima de la colina de Les Menes. Sólo se habían construido dos viviendas, la casa muestra, según proyecto de Francesc Berenguer, que acabó ocupando el propio Gaudí, y la que había encargado Martí Trias i Domènech al arquitecto Juli Batllevell i Arús (1864-1928). Eusebi Güell, por su parte, se había hecho restaurar y acondicionar la antigua casa Larrard, hoy en día reconvertida en escuela, resguardada bajo la gran explanada. Los herederos Güell, constituidos en una empresa, lo vendieron al Ayuntamiento de Barcelona, y en 1926 fue abierto como parque público.

Los pabellones de la entrada, el muro de cierre, la gran escalinata y los viaductos

Accedemos al Park, flanqueados por los dos edificios de servicio, hasta una pequeña plaza en donde nace la magnífica escalinata del dragón, que deja entrever más arriba la galería dórica o sala hipóstila. Al entrar, tenemos la sensación de que nos introducimos en un gran decorado escenográfico, con las dos casitas a lado y lado que presentan unas esplendorosas cubiertas de bóveda tabicada revestidas de trencadís cerámico. La casa orientada al este, la vivienda del guarda, está coronada con una caprichosa seta que parece una venenosa *Amanita muscaria*, en la que pueden verse piezas de porcelana doméstica que le aportan nuevos tonos y texturas. El otro pabellón, destinado a servicios para los habitantes de la urbanización, termina con una torre rematada con una cruz de cuatro brazos, como la que hará en Bellesguard cinco años más tarde. Muchas piezas cerámicas del revestimiento de estas cubiertas conservan el dibujo original, e incluso su forma y tamaño, pero fragmentadas. También podemos apreciar que hay una tendencia a emplear fragmentos relativamente pequeños y ordenados como corresponde a la etapa en que se construyen, antes de 1903.

Como urbanización aislada necesitaba un muro de cierre que, quizás, estaba previsto que rodeara toda la finca aunque sólo se construyó en el acceso principal. Está hecho en mampostería común y acabado con unos paneles cerámicos que alternan los colores rojo y blanco. Pero lo más destacado son unos grandes medallones hechos con moldes en los que se inscriben alternativamente las palabras «Park» y «Güell».

La plazoleta de acceso da paso a una escalinata que lleva hacia la sala hipóstila y la plaza superior. Los muros que la flanquean, cubiertos con cerámica de trencadís, simulan un gran escaqueado de grandes cuadrados de colores y rectángulos de fondo blanco. La parte superior culmina con unas terrazas acabadas con unas almenas de trencadís con una franja de color. En estas piezas hay una tendencia a deshacer los dibujos originales de los azulejos y a recrear otros nuevos, pero utilizando el mismo modelo, sin mezclar tipologías de dibujos.

La escalinata está organizada en tres tramos coronados por el dragón —o salamandra— que se ha convertido en la imagen más popular del parque. El dragón sobresale por encima de una fuente con el escudo de Cataluña inscrito dentro de un círculo de tonos azules con pequeñas incrustaciones circulares en relieve; el rebosadero de dicha fuente es la cabeza de un animal de difícil identificación, tal vez un perro. El dragón, que también derrama agua por la boca, a pesar de estar muy restaurado, mantiene la imagen y los colores originales, excepto en la disposición de las garras y en la desaparición casi total de los dientes. En el último tramo de la escalinata, resguardado bajo la sala hipóstila, hay un banco de planta semicircular de trencadís blanco rodeado por una gran franja verde y medallones de relieve con motivos florales en tonos ocres y terrosos.

Por último, hay que hacer una referencia al recubrimiento de piedra de los viaductos y los muros de contención, en *opus lithostrotum*, en la línea de lo que ya hemos visto en la Torre Bellesguard, edificio contemporáneo a esta obra. La estructura de viaductos y muros de contención, como se puede demostrar a partir de fotografías antiguas, está elaborada a partir de la clásica bóveda tabicada, con un recubrimiento de piedra vista sin desbastar, que a veces dibuja formas caprichosas en trencadís pétreo. Se utilizan acabados que simulan sillares regulares —como en el caso del viaducto del Medio—, aunque, en su mayoría, son de piedra sin pulir. En algunos casos, además, adoptan formas abstractas de gran belleza formal, como el diseño helicoidal que culmina, a modo de grandes capiteles, de las columnas de la rampa situada detrás de la Casa Güell; las piedras que simulan caer en forma de lluvia sobre la misma rampa; el juego de cuadrados y rectángulos, delimitados con guijarros blancos de la bóveda del viaducto del Medio o las formas triangulares en el caso del viaducto de Arriba. También se dibujan formas inspiradas en la naturaleza, como las palmeras que pueden verse en el muro de contención que bordea la gran explanada, y que entran en diálogo con las reales —plantadas ya en ese primer momento. El caso más popular, sin embargo, en el uso del mosaico pétreo, lo podemos apreciar en la escultura antropomórfica de la Lavandera, conocida con este nombre porque lleva los atributos de este oficio, un gran cesto sobre la cabeza con la colada y una pala de picar ropa en la mano derecha, que se había perdido y recientemente se ha restaurado. Según la fuente oral recogida por Joan Bassegoda en *El Gran Gaudí* (1989), esta figura fue realizada por el hijo de Agustín Massip, uno de los albañiles del Park.

La sala hipóstila, del trencadís blanco a la creatividad de Josep M. Jujol

La gran escalinata de acceso conduce a la sala hipóstila —o sala de las columnas—, que estaba destinada a ser el mercado de la urbanización, formada por 84 columnas estriadas y coronada por un entablamento sobre el que se emplaza el banco ondulado. La sala está cubierta por pequeñas cúpulas construidas como las bóvedas tabicadas, recubiertas de trencadís blanco.

Lo más destacado de la sala son los plafones, a modo de claves de bóveda, situados en unos espacios más amplios del techo que son resultado de la eliminación de columnas en algunos tramos. La dirección de la obra es de Josep M. Jujol, que propone unas piezas de extraordinaria originalidad en las que la aplicación de la cerámica se alterna con el vidrio como material principal, como ya hemos visto en las chimeneas del Palau Güell y en la cruz, coetánea, de Bellesguard. Aquí, sin embargo, coinciden un arquitecto que quiere aplicar una serie de materiales inusuales, Gaudí, con otro que tiene una capacidad de expresión fuera de lo normal, Jujol. El resultado es el sumatorio extraordinario de volúmenes y colores. Esta relación, según Carlos Flores, se inició gracias a Jaume Bayó, hermano del constructor de la Casa Batlló y de quien Jujol había sido discípulo en la Escuela de Arquitectura (Flores, 2002).

Estos plafones o medallones de la sala hipóstila, en el centro, representan unos soles de veinte puntas con colores y texturas distintas. Los acompañan, como si fueran antiguas claves de bóveda, en medio de las cúpulas que rodean los plafones, unas originales lunas, en número de catorce. Como son cuatro soles, podemos interpretar que hay uno por cada estación del año. Aunque parten del mismo diseño de base, el contraste entre los colores y materiales empleados en el trencadís, los hace a todos diferentes. Los medallones son de ladrillo prefabricado revestidos con unas texturas insólitas y variadísimas de materiales: vidrio, restos de vajilla doméstica, mosaico hidráulico, tapones de botellas de licor, frascos de perfumes, etc. La reciente restauración (2016) ha permitido volver a poder apreciarlos en todo su esplendor. Indudablemente, fueron realizados con la técnica directa, es decir, la aplicación de los materiales sobre el mortero fresco.

Los elementos vivenciales —el plato plano, el de sopa o el porrón de cristal rotos— que Jujol aplicará en 1914 en la Casa Bofarull, Els Pallaresos, ya los había empezado a utilizar aquí; parece que se reconocen unos platos de la vajilla de la propia familia Jujol (Josep M. Jujol junior, 2017). La recogida de objetos rotos por las casas, se extendió también a los trabajadores del Park, que los aportaban a la obra, como si fueran huellas dactilares o firmas de aquellos que participaron en ella.

El banco ondulado, una sinfonía de texturas y colores

El punto culminante en el uso del trencadís en el Park Güell es el banco-barandilla de la gran explanada, una plaza artificial, en parte excavada en la roca, en parte suspendida sobre la sala hipóstila. Lo que tenía que ser la barandilla protectora de la plaza se convirtió en el banco ondulado. La decoración de este extraordinario elemento fue dirigida, entre 1910 y 1914, por Josep M. Jujol (Duran, 2006; Freixa, Leniz, 2018), pero hasta la década de 1970 no se reconoció su participación en este banco cerámico (Flores, 1974).

La estructura del banco ondulado está formada por bloques prefabricados de rasillas, los ladrillos que se utilizaban para hacer la bóveda catalana o tabicada. Cada tramo del banco está formado por dos piezas, la que forma el asiento y la del respaldo, aguantadas con una estructura interior metálica. Los bloques adoptan formas cóncavas y convexas, en relación a la disposición de las columnas de la sala inferior, formando series de cuatro u ocho módulos para adaptarse al ritmo de las susodichas columnas.

En cuanto al mosaico que se aplicaba al asiento y al respaldo, debemos suponer que se hacía *in situ*, una vez dispuestas las estructuras en su lugar. La decoración de cada módulo, según explica el hijo de Jujol (Josep M. Jujol junior, 1974) —aunque se trata de un recuerdo oral que debemos recoger con la prudencia necesaria— se comenzaba por el reverso del respaldo, mientras que el anverso y la parte del asiento se elaboraban posteriormente.

Según este mismo testigo, trabajaban al mismo tiempo el arquitecto, un albañil y dos peones. Las carretadas de cerámica se dejaban en medio de la plaza y se iban seleccionando los fragmentos para hacer las composiciones. Esto responde a un hecho lógico: el trabajo se tenía que hacer en la misma obra para evitar el coste del traslado de piezas (Josep M. Jujol junior, 1974). Este sistema de taller en la propia obra también lo usaron los mosaiquistas que trabajaron en el Palau de la Música Catalana o en el Hospital de la Santa Creu i Sant Pau (Saliné, 2015). Recogemos una anécdota sobre la rotura de piezas en la que, una vez más, quizás al azar provocó un giro a favor de la utilización del trencadís. Según nos comenta Àngels López i Fusté, hija del delineante Francisco López i Sarasa, un día llegó un carro de cerámica al Park, y por accidente una importante cantidad de azulejos se rompieron. En ese momento, Eusebi Güell estaba en la obra y pudo ver el estropicio, y por lo tanto también un dinero perdido. Enfadado por el hecho, se quejó en voz alta pero Gaudí le contestó: «no se preocupe, que esto será una obra de arte». Desafortunadamente no podemos verificar mejor el dato, pero en todo caso el comentario nos llevaría a pensar que aquellos fragmentos serían una obra de arte o ayudarían a crearla.

Todos los dibujos de los mosaicos del banco se concebían y se producían a medida que se iban uniendo los materiales fragmentados y, en consecuencia, a partir de un gran número de manos anónimas. De ahí la diversidad de diseños. Esto no quiere decir que fuera una producción automática. Es muy posible que existiera un borrador inicial pero el dibujo surgía y se corregía a medida que se iban generando los fragmentos. Tampoco podemos olvidar la gran capacidad de Josep M. Jujol para el dibujo: en la Escuela de Arquitectura hacía dibujos de manera espontánea: «Jujol dibujaba con gran rapidez y precisión» (Correa, 1988). Esta habilidad, seguramente, fue utilizada en todas las obras en las que colaboró con Gaudí. Asimismo, sabemos por fuentes orales que Gaudí hacía un pequeño examen para ver las aptitudes de los trabajadores, y cuando mostraban sentido decorativo los ponía a realizar revestimientos de trencadís.

En general, podemos afirmar que las composiciones de trencadís de aspecto espontáneo, abstracto y en movimiento están previamente razonadas y no tanto realizadas al azar como pueda parece a primera vista.

En particular, en cuanto a la ornamentación de los elementos del banco (asiento y respaldo), sorprende por su gran riqueza la parte posterior del respaldo, a pesar de que es difícil de ver: alrededor de los desagües de evacuación del agua del asiento frontal, se crean unas composiciones que, a pesar de partir de un esquema similar, ofrecen resultados muy diferentes por el contraste de texturas y colores. Del orificio de cada desagüe surgen cinco ondeantes tallos enmarcados dentro de una especie de medallones de formas diferentes. Se nota una evolución hacia un uso más libre de los materiales con la progresiva incorporación de fragmentos de relieve y de todo tipo de elementos, o definiendo una línea de continuidad entre los medallones con dibujos e incrustaciones de todo tipo de componentes.

La zona frontal del banco está dividida en dos partes: la del asiento y la del respaldo. Es en este último elemento donde encontramos la mayor mezcla de materiales y, si la parte posterior del banco ya sorprende por la riqueza de sus diseños, la parte frontal asombra por la esplendorosa creatividad en el empleo de distintas tipologías de trencadís y diseños de colocación, tamaños, formas y materiales de los fragmentos, que se anticipan conceptualmente a las vanguardias del siglo XX en el uso de técnicas como el collage o de movimientos artísticos como la abstracción o el *arte povera* (arte pobre).

Los elementos de separación entre asiento y respaldo son unas piezas redondeadas, de media caña —especialmente diseñadas para el banco— de tonos verdes, amarillos y algunas con tonalidades azules. El tipo de pintado responde a la cerámica producida por la alfarería tradicional en las piezas vidriadas, como los platos y las ollas de consumo popular, o, en arquitectura, las tejas, por ejemplo. Aquí, el elemento se utiliza como línea continua separadora de los dos espacios decorados: está situada estratégicamente en el nacimiento del respaldo y con la idea de crear un elemento ergonómico. Las formas de las piezas no terminan en ángulos rectos, sino que tienen un acoplamiento sesgado en zigzag.

Existe aún otra línea de estas piezas de media caña en la parte superior del respaldo. Sirve como remate del banco y evita la entrada de agua en el interior de la estructura. Hay unas tipologías establecidas, tanto en las piezas de la línea superior como en las de la inferior, que se van repitiendo a lo largo de la ondulación y que están calculadas para encajar unas con otras.

Por otra parte, estas piezas de media caña —las originales que todavía encontramos *in situ* tras las restauraciones nos permiten apreciarlo— esconden otra sorpresa: unas sutiles marcas e inscripciones que aluden a la devoción mariana de Jujol. Fueron identificadas en 1964 por Josep Garganté y Santiago Loperena (Casanelles, 1965), y dibujadas y descritas por Joan Matamala (Bassegoda, 1986). Diez años más tarde, Carlos Flores encontraba la firma de Jujol entre las marcas, prueba inequívoca del gran peso que este tuvo en la ornamentación del banco (Flores, 1974). Con unas incisiones muy precisas, como si las marcaran con bisturí, vemos dibujos como pequeñas flores y otros motivos vegetales, una corona de espinas, etc., muchos de ellos ornamentando una preciosa caligrafía con frases marianas, escritas en latín o catalán: «Angelus domini nunciavit Maria» (El ángel le dijo a María), «Tum serveixes» (Tu me sirves), «Amb ella via de pau» (Con ella vía de paz), «Sos ulls» (Sus ojos). También hay alguna referencia a Jesús: «Rex» (Rey). Como nos recuerda el hijo de Jujol (Josep M. Jujol junior, 1974), este clamor mariano aparece escondido, camuflado dentro del juego de colores del banco, para no hacerlo demasiado evidente en una ciudad que, sólo tres años antes, había vivido un período revolucionario como el de la Semana Trágica. Las inscripciones se encuentran en piezas creadas de nuevo para el banco, y el mismo Jujol las habría grabado antes de la cocción, cuando el barro era blando. La confianza de Gaudí en Jujol para esta tarea era infinita, tal como han manifestado muchos testigos directos. El hecho de que las expresiones marianas y demás incisiones se hicieran sobre las piezas de barro blando antes de la cocción, deja claro que esta cerámica fue encargada y tratada durante el proceso de realización del banco.

El banco-barandilla del Park Güell se ha convertido en una obra emblemática para entender la concepción de la arquitectura de Antoni Gaudí y de Josep M. Jujol: innovación estructural unida a extraordinarios recursos en la aplicación del trencadís, y es, además, el mejor ejemplo de la colaboración entre ambos arquitectos.

El Park Güell, el gran catálogo del trencadís en Cataluña

No hay duda de que nos encontramos ante el mayor repertorio de trencadís producido por Gaudí. Este elemento que no plantea ninguna base geométrica y parece una simple deconstrucción de materiales nos engaña totalmente. Detrás de estas formas redondeadas hay unos cálculos de gran precisión: los cuadrados de la escalinata, las piezas creadas con moldes para hacer los remates (como las pequeñas almenas que coronan los muros de la escalinata o de las terrazas de los pabellones, los plafones de la muralla exterior...), el elemento de media caña del banco, etc. Así, el azar queda relegado a la rotura de las piezas y a la distribución decorativa de los dibujos, que parten de las manos de aquellos que los han elaborado, desde un Josep M. Jujol hasta un operario. Pero sobre todo, lo que vemos es geometría perfectamente calculada, aunque eso sí, escondida.

Respecto de los proveedores de materiales para confeccionar el trencadís, no podemos pensar sólo en un acopio de cerámica o vidrio basada en piezas de rechazo, aunque es evidente que Gaudí recoge elementos industriales de poco coste, como han ido desvelando varios autores y los estudios realizados por el Ayuntamiento de Barcelona para hacer las restauraciones (Subias, 1999, 2006; Duran, 2006). En el Park Güell, como en muchas otras obras del arquitecto, también se adquieren en los proveedores usuales y se compran piezas hechas por encargo.

El gran repertorio del trencadís cerámico del Park nos lleva a catalogarlo, en una primera aproximación, en los siguientes tipos básicos a partir de los cuales se generan múltiples combinaciones:

- Trencadís monocromo a veces con cambios de tonalidad.
- Trencadís monocromo en el que se insertan formas, bien monocromas bien policromas con dibujos abstractos.
- Trencadís policromo que fragmenta una o más piezas del mismo modelo volviéndolas a recomponer para obtener otra vez el diseño original.
- Trencadís policromo que fragmenta una o más piezas del mismo modelo pero que crean un nuevo dibujo cuando las vuelven a combinar.
- Trencadís policromo, generalmente abstracto, que sirve de fondo a un elemento (dibujo o relieve figurativo) que se pretende enaltecer.
- Trencadís policromo, que incluye objetos cotidianos de materiales diversos, ejemplo de collage y de arte pobre antes de que los formalizaran las vanguardias.

La Casa Batlló

El fragmento, unidad del elemento orgánico

Cronología: 1904-1907

Promotor: Josep Batlló i Casanovas

Localización: Passeig de Gràcia, 43. Barcelona

Tipología y uso: edificio de viviendas, reforma

Colaboradores: Francesc Berenguer i Mestres (1866-1914), Josep Canaleta i Cuadras (1875-1950), Domènec Sugrañes i Gras (1878-1938), Josep M. Jujol i Gibert (1879-1949)

Cerámica: Sebastià Ribó, Barcelona; La Roqueta, Palma; Nolla, València

Vidrio de la fachada: Tallers Pelegrí

Declaración de Bien Cultural del Patrimonio Mundial de la UNESCO (2005)

«Los colores usados en arquitectura han de ser intensos, lógicos y fértiles»

Antoni Gaudí (según Eusebi Casanelles, *Nueva visión de Gaudí*, 1965)

Si el Park Güell representa un gran catálogo de sistemas de aplicación, la Casa Batlló es, en todo su conjunto, como un fragmento dibujado o aplicado en trencadís y en otras técnicas. Atrás quedan las formas originales geométricas, que se transforman en diseños sinuosos y redondeados que imitan el color y la morfología de la naturaleza.

El edificio de vecinos proyectado por Gaudí es la reforma de uno anterior construido por Emili Sala i Cortés (1841-1921) en 1877. Su fachada frontal, de vidrio y cerámica, es la más impactante de todo el Modernismo catalán. Sobre el mismo paramento vertical, encontramos producciones de cerámica vidriada, discos de diferentes tamaños, que se alternan con fragmentos de vidrio. El resultado de la aplicación es tan interesante que la parte superior de los ventanales siguen también la imagen de la fachada: vitrales con cibas y fragmentos de diferentes tamaños y colores.

Tenemos un testimonio muy importante para conocer el proceso constructivo, el de Josep Bayó i Font (1878-1971), constructor y ejecutor de la reforma, quien fue entrevistado, en 1970, por Joan Bassegoda i Nonell (Bassegoda, 2003), ahora recogido en el Plan Director para las intervenciones de la Casa Batlló (Onecha, Bosch, Olona, Dotor, 2017). En la fachada principal, revestida de vidrios de colores y discos cerámicos de diferentes tamaños, Bayó explica que Gaudí daba las instrucciones «de viva voz», y añade: «él nos decía, a aquella aguja denle un trozo en verde; aquella punta me la acaban en verde, y aquí en azul. Y, como ya teníamos la pared enlucida y fratasada, entonces con cemento *griffi* extendíamos el trozo que pensábamos hacer durante esas dos o cuatro horas de trabajo». La descripción nos indica que se aplicaba la técnica directa. Durante el tiempo en que el cemento estaba blando, se podían asentar sobre el mortero los cristales e ir igualando los fragmentos insertados nivelándolos para que no sobresalieran del conjunto. Bayó añade que Gaudí siempre les decía: «no acaben carrat» (truncado, cortado en la punta), «acaben siempre en cristal puntiagudo, para que combine con otro». Si recordamos la técnica de producción del mosaico, los remates eran dentados para simular las uniones. Ahora Gaudí nos presenta la misma imagen con los fragmentos de vidrio creando zigzags dentados. La torre de esta fachada tiene adheridos en cerámica dorada de relieve los monogramas de la Sagrada Familia de Nazaret: de abajo a arriba en ascendencia helicoidal, José (JHP), María (M coronada) y Jesús (IHS).

El remate de la torre, una exuberante forma bulbosa y la cruz de cuatro brazos, está segmentado. La pieza se rompió durante la cocción en el horno, pero Gaudí la recupera de todas maneras y la aplica como magnífico coronamiento. Si no se conociera esta anécdota, podría parecer que el fragmentado lo había proyectado el propio arquitecto. Por tradición oral (Bassegoda, 1978; Flores, 1982) se cree que es una producción de la fábrica de cerámica *La Roqueta*, de Palma. La fachada principal termina con una espectacular mansarda ondulada, cubierta con una especie de escamas, coronada por unas monumentales piezas de cerámica similares a las de media caña de color tostado, con otras piezas sobrepuestas de tonos verdes y azules, y que, según el Plan Director se pueden atribuir a Sebastià Ribó. Esta mansarda, por la parte que da a la fachada posterior, está revestida de trencadís cerámico con una degradación de color que va del marrón al blanco.

Subir por la escalera de vecinos, alicatada de cerámica blanca y azul que modula los tonos en función de la luz que recibe (más oscura cuanta más luz, más clara cuanta menos), es una experiencia irrepetible. Las piezas azules son del taller de Ribó, como se ha podido comprobar en las inscripciones del reverso. Los ángulos se revistieron a partir de fragmentos de la misma cerámica cortados de forma regular con punta de diamante; de este modo, en lugar de terminar en simple arista, crean una media caña. Son pequeños detalles que pueden pasar desapercibidos pero que explican el cuidado con que se hacían los acabados.

La azotea merece una descripción especial. Los tendederos quedaban escondidos en el desván, donde las corrientes de aire estaban controladas y la ropa estaba protegida de la lluvia, por lo que la azotea tenía una función lúdica al servicio de los habitantes del inmueble. El doble acceso de salida de la escalera y los conjuntos de chimeneas, a pesar de tener funciones diferenciadas, mantienen una imagen homogénea. Evocan el aspecto de unas setas de cepa gigantescas: sobre una base común surgen las chimeneas decoradas con cristal y coronadas por sombreretes con fondo de cristal y cerámica que recrean elementos florales muy estilizados. Algunos de los pétalos podrían estar realizados a partir de azulejos recortados o marcados con punta de diamante ya que no muestran un corte al azar y tienen tamaños y formas muy similares y repetitivos. Se puede apreciar también algún cristal de claraboya recuperado, que siempre se enganchaba al mortero por el lado de las rugosidades, ya que así se favorecía la sujeción, y la transparencia del cristal permitía apreciar el dibujo. Estos elementos de cubierta estaban coronados, inicialmente, según recuerda Bayó (Bassegoda, 2003), por bolas de cristal con arena de colores o mortero coloreado.

El pavimento de la azotea, hoy desaparecido, también era de trencadís, pero de un trencadís muy especial (Bosch, Olona, 2017), ya que se utilizaron los restos de baldosines de gres de los pavimentos de los pisos del edificio preexistente, reciclando nuevamente, como en obras anteriores, los materiales disponibles. Los obreros los limpiaron del mortero del reverso y los soladores los volvieron a colocar. Estos baldosines eran realmente muy duros, así que no era práctico romperlos, además de ser muy pequeños, aproximadamente unos 4 × 4 cm. El pavimento de gres, sobre todo si se trataba de la producción de la casa Nolla de Valencia, necesitaba de mosaiquistas especializados para colocar las piezas. La complejidad geométrica de los dibujos y la colocación con técnica directa tesela a tesela complicaba los procesos. Pero aquí, Gaudí se ahorró la compra de los materiales y también la mano de obra especializada. En este espacio, el arquitecto no buscó el dibujo reproducido por los catálogos, sino nuevos modelos surgidos del proceso de colocación de sus operarios, a quienes sin duda consideraba cualificados para realizar formas y dibujos maravillosos sin necesidad de guía. Bayó dice (Bassegoda, 2003) que Gaudí comentó a los operarios: «del dibujo no se preocupen, será el que sea», una extraordinaria frase que podríamos extrapolar a todo el trencadís.

Sobre la fachada posterior, la primera consideración es que no se trata de una fachada secundaria, ya que el propietario la disfrutaba desde el jardín del piso principal. El mosaico mantiene una temática de continuidad con los elementos dibujados en la azotea. Toda la fachada es una evocación de la naturaleza a partir de la representación de formas florales muy estilizadas, alternándolas con modelos geométricos. También cabe destacar la composición a partir de unos ejes de simetría muy cuidados, que dan como resultado un diseño meticuloso, nada anárquico, que incluso repite los mismos esquemas. Es un concepto muy diferente de la fachada principal donde los colores de los cristales y la creación de tornasolados es el elemento dominante. Gaudí proyectó un primer grupo de mosaicos en el coronamiento superior que actúa como elemento de protección, como una barandilla. El mismo modelo tiene continuidad debajo mismo, integrando la barandilla del balcón corrido de la buhardilla, que se estructura a partir de catorce pequeñas aberturas redondas con un centro triangular. Por debajo de estas aberturas, se desarrolla una magnífica cenefa de flores con diseños repetitivos y con pétalos blancos. Además, verticalmente, hay dos tiras de mosaico a ambos lados de la fachada que cuelgan como una guirnalda desde el coronamiento hasta llegar al patio del piso principal. Este elemento está formado por una serie de círculos de diferentes tamaños que contienen flores de ricos colores y formas totalmente nuevas.

El patio exterior del piso principal, como resultado de la reforma emprendida por Gaudí, es de hecho un lugar de descanso definido por un espacio ajardinado visible desde el comedor. El pavimento dibuja una franja central de pequeñas piezas de gres que iba desde la abertura central de la casa hasta el fondo del patio, donde hay una jardinera inscrita en un arco parabólico hecho de trencadís y de las mismas piezas circulares de la fachada principal. Según antiguas fotografías, esta franja estaba cubierta con una pérgola o umbráculo con la misma forma parabólica que acabamos de mencionar, y que tenía como función asegurar la intimidad de los propietarios respecto del resto de vecinos. A ambos lados de la franja, también se dispone pavimento *Nolla*, aunque en los cuatro extremos se coloca formando trencadís, como en la azotea. Todo el conjunto fue restaurado durante los años noventa del siglo pasado.

La Casa Batlló está configurada como una composición de células. El vidrio y la cerámica de las dos fachadas, los remates, pero también los azulejos del patio de luces, son como un gran mosaico. Encontramos también la huella del fragmento en los cristales ondulantes de la escalera, o en el pintado al fuego con dorados del piso principal. Así no es difícil pensar que la imagen y la forma del fragmento y del trencadís son el elemento principal de este edificio.

Casa Milà Segimon, La Pedrera

La forma por encima del color

Cronología: 1906-1912

Promotores: Roser Segimon de Milà y Pere Milà i Camps

Localización: Passeig de Gràcia, 92. Barcelona

Tipología y uso: edificio de viviendas de nueva planta

Colaboradores: Josep Canaleta i Cuadras (1875-1950), Josep M. Jujol i Gibert (1879-1949), Domènec Sugrañes i Gras (1878-1938)

Material pétreo: piedra de Ulldecona y variantes de Sénia, Xert o Borriol; mármol tipo Macael, Tranco o Carrara (Asarta, 1998)

El vidrio verde: botellas de uso común a principios del siglo XX

Declaración de Bien Cultural del Patrimonio Mundial de la UNESCO (1984)

«Los paraboloides, hiperboloides y helicoides, variando constantemente la incidencia de la luz, tienen una riqueza propia de matices, que hacen innecesaria la ornamentación»

Antoni Gaudí (según Joan Bergós, *Gaudí, l'home i l'obra*, 1954)

Si bien el color es muy importante en la arquitectura de Gaudí, la forma y el conocimiento profundo de la geometría le llevan a crear una arquitectura siempre en movimiento que genera formas extraordinarias. La utilización del trencadís en la azotea de La Pedrera, que rompe con los cromatismos experimentados anteriormente, plantea una nueva lectura basada en el uso de un solo color, una monocromía que refuerza el sentido expresivo a partir de las ondulaciones y relieves del conjunto, formas que, en la distancia, se ven esculpidas y no revestidas.

La Pedrera es una construcción de nueva planta que ocupa una gran esquina del Passeig de Gràcia con la calle Provença y da cabida a dos edificios de viviendas. Los promotores eran Pere Milà i Camps y su esposa, Roser Segimon, viuda de Josep Guardiola i Grau, de quien Roser heredó una gran fortuna que, en gran parte, usó para construir este suntuoso edificio. La construcción de la Casa Milà se inicia en 1906 y se estuvo trabajando hasta 1912. Es una obra monumental que, ya en la época, superaba toda normativa municipal. Lo primero que se aprecia desde el exterior es la potencia de su fachada de piedra —que le ha otorgado el nombre popular de La Pedrera— pero la casa esconde muchos secretos, el trabajo en hierro, la pintura mural y también el revestimiento en trencadís.

Para descubrir este último aspecto, podemos proponer dos aproximaciones, interpretar el edificio desde su exterior y la visión cercana de los elementos desde la misma azotea. Desde la calle, sobresalen las grandes cajas de escalera, blancas sobre la masa pétrea, en contraste con la gran cornisa de piedra lisa. Son unos elementos que contribuyen a materializar la armonía del conjunto con la sabia vibración y contraste de los materiales empleados, cerámica y mármol. En un plano inferior, hay un estrecho «camino de ronda» en cuyos extremos presenta unas tribunas cubiertas con pequeñas cúpulas de trencadís cerámico blanco, que tienen como objetivo definir el ritmo ondulante de la cubierta, enmarcando las inscripciones latinas del avemaría grabadas en altorrelieve de piedra. El espacio central del coronamiento estaría reservado para un grupo escultórico de la Virgen del Rosario que nunca fue realizado.

Si subimos a la azotea, encontramos diversidad de elementos con trencadís, herencia de la experiencia aplicada en el Palau Güell, con un posible precedente cromático, y en la Casa Batlló. Los tendederos, como en esta última, quedan escondidos en el desván, así que, nuevamente, se trata de hacer un proyecto de organización y orden del espacio. Los elementos más representativos son las seis cajas de escalera, cuatro revestidas de trencadís y las otras dos suavemente coloreadas de ocre con un estucado de mortero, de yeso y de cal. Los últimos estudios de los conservadores del edificio se inclinan a pensar que, en origen, todos los elementos tenían que estar cubiertos de materiales impermeables y que, finalmente, por los costes de la construcción, sólo se revistieron los elementos más grandes y visibles desde la calle.

Las cajas de escalera están revestidas con diferentes materiales, cerámica, mármol o piedra de múltiples tonos blancos. Las dos más visibles desde la calle están proyectadas de manera independiente. Están coronadas por cruces en las cuatro caras, con la parte visible de forma cóncava, desde la que se desarrolla una franja que se desliza en movimiento helicoidal hasta la base. Los materiales se aplican de manera independiente. La cara de la cruz emplea trencadís de cerámica vidriada mientras que la otra es de fragmentos de piedra y mármol sin pulir, un sistema sorprendente por la riqueza de texturas y contrastes. Las otras cuatro repiten volumetría, dos con revestimiento y las otras dos sin. Todas están coronadas con referencias a la cruz, por un lado una cruz acolchada y por el otro, un círculo dividido por formas cóncavas que generan la misma cruz. Las formas de los cuatro modelos están especialmente pensadas para facilitar el drenaje del agua de lluvia y la autolimpieza en el caso de las que tienen revestimiento.

Yendo al detalle se ofrece otro nivel de lectura. Mirando muy de cerca el rompecabezas del revestimiento de trencadís se descubren inscripciones y marcas sorprendentes, objetos elegidos al azar —muchos de ellos con su propia historia—, fragmentos de piedra provenientes de la fachada, mármoles sin pulir, trozos de cerámica con diversidad de errores de cocción, goteos de barnices, cocciones a demasiada temperatura, suciedad antes de esmaltar, etc.

En la misma cubierta, destaca también el conjunto de chimeneas —que la literatura popular ha definido como «guerreros»—, de las que sólo un grupo, el situado más hacia el norte, lleva un original revestimiento de vidrio verde. Está hecho a base de fragmentos de botella y alguna contada aplicación en cerámica de color blanco. Este toque de color en vidrio tiene un largo recorrido en las obras previas hasta llegar aquí, pero las anteriores aplicaciones creaban un revestimiento con el vidrio plano sobre el mortero, mientras que aquí se clava el fragmento de vidrio. Por la factura, recuerda la tradición de clavar cristales de colores en lo más alto de las tapias para dificultar la entrada de intrusos. Esta intervención se ha atribuido a la colaboración de Josep M. Jujol (Josep M. Jujol junior, 1974), ya que era contemporánea de la que hizo en los medallones de la sala hipóstila del Park Güell.

Se puede concluir con la convicción de que La Pedrera descubre las posibilidades cromáticas de un color que no es color, el blanco. Diferentes materiales, el mármol, la piedra y la complejidad de obtener un blanco homogéneo en la cerámica, están en la base de esta pluralidad. El color blanco era uno de los más difíciles de conseguir, según comenta el ceramista y restaurador Manuel Diestre, debido a que con la base del esmalte, se mezclaba ceniza y tierra del horno. Cuando se mezclaba con el estaño base de la baldosa, siempre daba diferentes tonalidades de blancos. Una producción ideal para un Gaudí tan amigo de las sincronías al azar.

La iglesia de la Colonia Güell

La relevancia de los materiales esenciales

Cronología: 1898-1915

Promotor: Eusebi Güell i Bacigalupi

Localización: Colonia Güell. Santa Coloma de Cervelló

Tipología y uso: templo

Colaboradores: Francesc Berenguer i Mestres (1866-1914), Josep Canaleta i Cuadras (1875-1950), Joan Rubió i Bellver (1870-1952) (en el proyecto urbanístico y en la construcción de otros edificios)

Cerámica: Josep Orriols, Barcelona; Ribalaiga Terrés i Mir, Barcelona; Vda. e Hijos de Juan Vila, Barcelona; Hijo de Jaime Pujol i Bausis, Esplugues de Llobregat

Declaración de Bien Cultural del Patrimonio Mundial de la UNESCO (2005)

«El templo ha de reunir la grandeza con la necesidad»

Antoni Gaudí (según Eusebi Casanelles, *Nueva visión de Gaudí*, 1965)

La belleza, la verdad, el esplendor religioso no necesitan grandeza económica, sino calidad espiritual. Y, para alcanzarla, Gaudí proyecta un templo pequeño para una colonia obrera y recupera todo tipo de productos, algunos de ellos muy deteriorados. Se aplican en un espacio místico de adoración como si toda la materia, cualquiera que sea y más allá de su estado, pudiera convertirse en esencial.

La colonia había sido fundada por Eusebi Güell en 1890, cuando trasladó la actividad del Vapor Vell de Sants con el objetivo de crear un espacio de trabajo en el que dominara la paz social. La fábrica y la urbanización —con todos los inmuebles necesarios, viviendas dignas, pero también, escuela y casa del maestro, cooperativa, local social, teatro, etc.— fueron realizadas por colaboradores directos de Gaudí, quien se reservó la construcción del templo. Estuvo diez años, entre 1898 y 1908, para trazar el complejo proyecto del templo y, una vez iniciadas las obras, estuvo trabajando hasta el mes de octubre de 1914. Después, la obra se continuó hasta que se inauguró, inacabada, el año siguiente. Gaudí abandonó las obras a la vez que dejaba también las del Park Güell y, a partir de esa fecha, sólo se dedicó a la Sagrada Familia. El proyecto de Gaudí contemplaba un templo con dos naves superpuestas, pero sólo se edificó la baja, que se conoce como cripta, aunque debemos aclarar que no es una cripta en sentido estricto, ya que este tipo de edificación siempre está ubicada entre los cimientos de la construcción superior, por debajo del nivel del suelo.

La iglesia muestra diferentes categorías de revestimiento. En primer lugar, toda una selección de materiales básicos y de buena calidad para la construcción, como el ladrillo y la piedra del entorno. En cambio, respecto de la aplicación del vidrio y la cerámica, sorprende la diversidad y la cantidad de materiales de desecho empleados, ladrillos, cerámicas vidriadas destruidas durante la producción hasta el punto de perder su función e incluso su apariencia, escoria de siderurgia, etc. También recoge materiales de las otras obras en curso, como señalan algunas anotaciones conservadas en el Archivo Parroquial de la colonia, según las cuales los carros transportaban, por ejemplo, materiales desde el Park Güell a Santa Coloma (Galí, Lacuesta, Micaló, 2004).

La aplicación del mosaico cerámico es uno de los revestimientos más elaborados del conjunto de elementos ornamentales de la iglesia y, además, disponemos de un estudio muy completo elaborado por técnicos de la Diputación de Barcelona (Galí, Lacuesta, Micaló, 2004). La gran aportación de los revestimientos de este templo es que muestra imágenes identificables de símbolos religiosos que sobresalen de la pared creados con el sistema de pequeño panel y la ya definida técnica indirecta. En cambio, en las anteriores obras, la temática del mosaico era esencialmente abstracto. Sólo podríamos encontrar como antecedente la fachada posterior de la Casa Batlló, pero allí la decoración es únicamente floral. En la iglesia de la colonia se pueden identificar muchos elementos cargados de simbolismo, como el alfa y el omega, es decir, el principio y el fin, o el estaurograma, la representación de la crucifixión de Cristo. También podemos ver un gran número de peces de colores, una de las representaciones más habituales desde el inicio del cristianismo, que parece como si nadasen a través de las paredes abruptas de la iglesia.

El elemento más representativo es el espléndido mosaico de vidrio y cerámica ubicado en el tímpano de acceso a la iglesia, bajo el gran porche de la entrada. Es un elemento de una provocadora modernidad que interpreta la iconografía cristiana junto a modelos locales aferrados a la cultura del territorio. Estos símbolos han sido estudiados en el proceso de restauración del templo (Galí, Lacuesta, Micaló, 2004). La parte central está formada por un dibujo octogonal, con el anagrama de la Trinidad, desde el que se desarrolla todo el resto de representaciones. A pesar de que ya han sido descritas en el trabajo citado, no podemos dejar de mencionar algunas imágenes como la antorcha que simboliza la fe y la luz; la plomada y la escuadra, símbolos de la construcción y que aquí se interpretan como la razón y la justicia; o el porrón de vino —la imagen de la moderación— que representa la templanza a través de un objeto común y tradicional en las casas catalanas. También se representan un gran número de elementos florales y vegetales, la hoja de olivo como significado de paz o la espina santa (*Paliurus spina-christi*), que recuerda la corona de espinas de Jesús. En algunas ocasiones hay diferencias de criterio a la hora de discernir los objetos representados.

También hay que mencionar el revestimiento de las bóvedas del porche, unos bellos paraboloides hiperbólicos. La morfología curvilínea de las bóvedas de la entrada crean formas redondeadas que están revestidas con piezas de arcilla sin barnizar. Lo primero que nos sorprende es la simetría del corte de las piezas utilizadas como revestimiento que nos recuerda las primeras intervenciones en los Pabellones Güell, no tanto por la aplicación del color como por los cortes simétricos y regulares de la tradición mudéjar. Los fragmentos están producidos a partir de rasillas sin barnizar utilizadas habitualmente como revestimiento de pavimentos de tejados y porches o bóvedas de las casas tradicionales y las masías. Aquí, Gaudí las hace cortar en cuatro triángulos. Los fragmentos de las rasillas crean una retícula ordenada de una singularidad y complejidad geométrica capital creando diferentes composiciones (González, 2004). La decoración de estos fragmentos sin vidriar trabajan como un fondo del que sobresale, en la parte central, una cruz de cerámica vidriada roja o negra; la cruz de San Andrés, que recuerda al mártir crucificado en una X de aspas iguales.

Otro elemento con mosaicos que hay que destacar son las ventanas, coloreadas con fragmentos de cerámica y vidrio y coronadas por mosaicos de cruces que sintetizan el estaurograma. Los revestimientos de las ventanas sobresalen brutalmente del muro, como si fueran un marco cromático para los vitrales. Nuevamente, el imaginario personal de cada observador puede plantear respuestas diferentes. ¿Tienen forma de llama? ¿Quizás de lágrima para evocar un desgraciado accidente de un joven trabajador? ¿De piñas, teniendo en cuenta que los vitrales representan piñas abiertas? Cada uno deberá forjarse su hipótesis. Aquí se recupera la imagen más tradicional del trencadís gaudiniano, pero cada ventana está tratada de forma individual. Reviste todos los elementos de la ventana, el intradós, los lados e incluso crea un pequeño remate para proteger la abertura. La cerámica aplicada pertenece, como en otras obras, a distintas empresas pero en esta destaca la procedente de la fábrica *Pujol i Bausis*.

En cuanto a la técnica, se utiliza tanto la directa como la indirecta. Los elementos de volumen se realizan con la indirecta sobre molde y los fragmentos para crear los colores son principalmente de vidrio. El revestimiento de las ventanas, en cambio, esta hecho con la técnica directa y con una gran diversidad de materiales cerámicos. Destaca la existencia de muchos azulejos en relieve y también escamas para cubiertas que en muchas ocasiones están cortadas en cuatro trozos que crean la forma de cruz. Encontramos la aplicación puntual de algunos azulejos de producciones del siglo XIX de 15 × 15 cm. Los estudios realizados por la Diputación de Barcelona indican la recuperación de piezas de la Torre Salvana, del siglo XVII (Lacuesta, 2004), antiguo castillo que se localiza justo en la entrada de la Colonia Güell. Sobre los diseños, por ejemplo, de las diecisiete ventanas habría que hacer un estudio particular por su diversidad.

Aunque se trata de una obra inacabada, podemos ver como la aplicación del trencadís ha evolucionado y plantea nuevas aportaciones. Se podría hablar de la presencia de los materiales que rezuman una esencia propia adquirida a partir de su historia y nos muestran el valor de la perdurabilidad. Gaudí nos dice: «la originalidad no se debe buscar» (Bergós, 1954) y la Colonia Güell es un continente de elementos fortuitos que produce la industria o la historia personal del elemento pero que en el último momento se convierten en parte del contexto constructivo y decorativo, más allá de la piel del edificio. Como si toda la materia, cualquiera que sea su forma, fuese esencial y esencia.

Y un punto final, la Sagrada Familia (1883-1926)

Cronología: 1883-1926

Promotor: Associació Espiritual de Devots de Sant Josep

Localización: Plaça de Gaudí. Barcelona

Tipología y uso: templo expiatorio

Colaboradores: Francesc Berenguer i Mestres (1866-1914), Josep M. Jujol i Gibert (1879-1949), Josep Francesc Ràfols i Fontanals (1889-1965), Cèsar Martinell i Brunet (1888-1973), Joan Bergós i Massó (1894-1974), Francesc Folguera i Grassi (1891-1960), Josep Canaleta i Cuadras (1875-1950), Joan Rubió i Bellver (1870-1952). Tras su muerte: Domènec Sugrañes i Gras (1878-1938), Isidre Puig i Boada (1891-1987), Lluís Bonet i Garí (1893-1993)

Fachada del Nacimiento: Declaración de Bien Cultural del Patrimonio Mundial de la UNESCO (2005)

«La belleza es el resplandor de la Verdad; y el resplandor seduce a todos, por eso el arte tiene universalidad»

Antoni Gaudí (según Marcià Codinachs, *Manuscritos, artículos, conversaciones y dibujos*, 1982)

El Gaudí religioso se percibe en su gran obra: el Templo Expiatorio de la Sagrada Familia. La identificación entre la belleza y la verdad enmarca la profunda religiosidad del arquitecto en la edad adulta, dedicado únicamente —en cuerpo y alma— a la Sagrada Familia. Gaudí sólo vio terminado el campanario de San Bernabé de la fachada del Nacimiento, pero estaba muy definida cómo debía ser la policromía del templo a partir de la maqueta que había en el taller. Cèsar Martinell, uno de sus últimos discípulos, describe los encuentros que tuvo con el arquitecto entre 1915 y 1926, incluyendo también las visitas que recibía de diferentes colectivos, y sorprende que, en más de una ocasión, las comenzara en el taller ante esta maqueta, justificando que la arquitectura tenía que ser policroma (Martinell, 1951). Realizada a escala 1:25, fue expuesta en París en 1910, en la exposición que ya hemos comentado. Jujol fue el encargado de hacer esta decoración que, ahora, tras una compleja restauración, se puede ver en el Museo de la Sagrada Familia. Actualmente, sólo está policromado el ciprés, rebosante de palomas, que corona el portal de la Caridad y que aún no estaba hecho cuando Gaudí murió, como se puede apreciar en las fotografías de época.

La aplicación del mosaico se reservaba preferentemente para los pináculos que rematan las torres, aunque podemos encontrar algunos otros detalles en color como la cruz que corona el ciprés. Martinell describe una visita a Gaudí el día 22 de enero de 1926, cuando el primer campanario estaba terminado. Este encuentro permite conocer muchos detalles sobre el punto en que se encontraba la construcción en ese momento (Martinell, 1951). Gaudí quiso aplicar el mosaico de más calidad y el más costoso, el mosaico de cristal veneciano que se encargó en la misma Venecia y que supuso un retraso de más de cuatro años. Se confeccionaba con vidrio ordinario verde, que es el más resistente, se ponía a fundir, y encima se extendía una hoja de pan de oro. El oro se funde a temperatura más baja, por lo que se integra en la superficie del vidrio. Así lo describe Martinell, pero sabemos que para consolidar el pan de oro sobre el vidrio veneciano, se necesita otro vidrio fino encima de esta película dorada y así se consigue un todo compacto. Los pináculos están dedicados a los obispos y representan las insignias episcopales. Tienen la forma del báculo y culminan con la mitra con la cruz inscrita. El anillo, por su parte, está representado por el vacío que se ve en la base de cada báculo.

Al inicio del pináculo, bajo los atributos de los obispos, hay unas letras en *opus tessellatum*, con teselas blancas. Están dispuestas verticalmente y tienen tamaños diferentes, mayores cuanto más arriba se encuentran. Componen, de arriba a abajo, las palabras en latín «Hosanna» y «Excelsis», separadas por unas franjas ornamentadas con la técnica del *opus spicatum*, que alternan piezas de ladrillo con otras de cerámica verde y roja. Todavía no estaban colocadas a principios de 1926, según Martinell, pero ya se pueden apreciar en las fotografías asociadas a la muerte de Gaudí, como la representación de la Santísima Trinidad sobre el ciprés, que tiene una cruz en forma de Tau, hecha también después de su muerte.

Podemos acabar con unas palabras de Gaudí, citadas por Bergós, que recogen la admiración del arquitecto por la belleza de un material que clarifica la significación del campanario, unir la tierra con el cielo y, al mismo tiempo, por la vistosidad del coronamiento que da la bienvenida a los navegantes que se acercan a la ciudad:

«¡Mire este final! ¿No es verdad que parece que una la tierra con el Cielo? Este estallido de mosaicos es lo primero que verán los navegantes al acercarse a Barcelona. ¡Será una radiante bienvenida!» (Bergós, 1954).

El rompecabezas del trencadís

¿Revestimiento a conservar o superficie de sacrificio?

Jaume Coll Conesa
Director del Museo Nacional de Cerámica
y de las Artes Suntuarias González Martí

Desde sus orígenes, la arquitectura ha buscado integrar el color en sus realizaciones. El color ha sido uno de sus componentes fundamentales y más visibles, hasta el punto que, con su pérdida, los aspectos sociales y simbólicos que este arte de síntesis encierra se ven seriamente penalizados por un fuerte menoscabo en su percepción.

El trencadís modernista tiene una función muy parecida a la cerámica. Aportaba forma y color sobre un despiece inusual que podríamos considerar el primer *repurposing* de un material cerámico. Bajo esta denominación incluimos también el llamado *collage*, definido como objetos desplazados de su función original para desarrollar otra diferente (Duran, 2006). No es reciclaje, es re-uso con nueva formulación plástica.

Podemos entonces definir algunas de las características esenciales del trencadís:

— Representa una creatividad singular de la mano de una concreta filosofía de la arquitectura que nace en un contexto social e histórico determinado.

— Su idea es fruto de un concepto de autor. Esta característica ya fue señalada por Alexandre Cirici al indicar que el collage aplicado en el banco del Park Güell no sólo lo convertía en una obra arquitectónica con un lenguaje particular sino también en obra pictórica (Duran, 2006). Su aplicación singular, caso a caso, se relaciona con dos agentes creativos: el arquitecto y el mosaiquista. El primero como autor de la obra concebida como un todo contenedor y de la visión y directrices que propone sobre las partes que la configuran; el segundo como autor de la ejecución del detalle creativo.

— Al formar parte de la complejidad de una estructura arquitectónica, manifiesta dos dependencias esenciales:

- Por una parte, es un elemento intencional de la propia expresividad de la obra así como de su identidad.
- Por otra, como elemento solidario de la primera, su preservación es consustancial a la del mismo bien sobre el que se aplica.

La subsidiariedad de estos elementos de la obra arquitectónica ya fue destacada por Antoni González, en la Mesa redonda del Congreso de Esplugues, como un elemento clave a la hora de tratar el edificio ya que participa de la obra como documento histórico, como objeto arquitectónico y como objeto simbólico y significativo para la sociedad, incluso hasta el punto de hacer que ese elemento pueda ser más importante que la propia arquitectura que lo sustenta (Mesa Redonda, 2006).

El uso innovador del material cerámico, y por ende del trencadís, chocó con un lastre ineludible que acompaña a la cerámica aplicada desde sus orígenes: la necesidad de utilizar una masa de agarre para su instalación. Los problemas asociados a las diferentes respuestas del material y los diferentes criterios y posibilidades de actuación para su conservación, ya fueron señalados en la sesión preliminar del encuentro del ICCROM y Academia de España en Roma sobre Estudio y Conservación sobre cerámica decorada aplicada a la Arquitectura (Almagro et al., 2001). En relación con el soporte, también interviene la estabilidad mecánica de la propia construcción, susceptible de ser alterada por humedades, desplazamientos, etc. En el caso de los elementos cerámicos, junto a su estrecha dependencia de esos aspectos técnico-constructivos, su perduración se relaciona con otros factores como la propia estabilidad estructural del material dependiente de sus características físicas: su naturaleza, su tenacidad, su dureza o su porosidad (Vendrell, 2003).

El primer aspecto posee una singular importancia, ya que la cerámica aplicada puede estar realizada con materiales que presentan unidad entre soporte y recubrimiento cromático, como ocurre en el gres, o por el contrario posee varias capas de naturaleza diferente, como ocurre en la mayólica, que combina un soporte arcilloso y un recubrimiento vítreo superpuesto. Antoni Cumella comentó, en la Mesa Redonda del congreso de Esplugues, la mayor o menor idoneidad de unos y otros productos cerámicos para su aplicación en exteriores (Mesa Redonda, 2006).

El gres, la porcelana, la loza dura o la tierra de pipa, tienen una menor porosidad abierta en comparación con la terracota o la mayólica. Las superficies vitrificadas basadas en la fusión superficial del cuerpo cerámico, como el gres a la sal o las cubiertas feldespáticas de porcelana, no poseen estructuras con comportamientos diferenciados frente a los fenómenos físicos externos. Sin embargo, en el caso de los vidrios aplicados sobre cuerpos cerámicos, en la mayólica o en la loza fina, el comportamiento no uniforme de base y cubierta ofrecerá una mayor complejidad en su conservación. En este caso puede darse una respuesta física diferente en la dilatación de cada una de las superficies, por ejemplo, o problemas de cohesión base-soporte que pudieron originarse en el momento de la propia fabricación del elemento cerámico por incorrectas formulaciones o cocciones. El comportamiento físico del material cerámico poroso con estructura multicapa es especialmente sensible al problema de la formación de sales en la superficie de contacto soporte-vidrio, muchas veces por la incorporación de éstas por sus capacidades higroscópicas —ambientes con aire salino por ejemplo—, al crecimiento de líquenes, musgos o especies vegetales de mayor porte, e incluso a las alteraciones mecánicas que pueden derivar de factores biológicos como termiteros, hormigueros, nidos de insectos o aves, etc. Las sales de los morteros de soporte pueden disolverse por la humedad y migrar hacia los elementos cerámicos penetrando en éstos si son porosos. Cuando emergiendo del cuerpo arcilloso entran en contacto con el vidrio debilitan la cohesión entre ambas superficies y provocan su separación. El propio mortero puede desintegrarse y ocasionar directamente desprendimientos de la capa de material cerámico.

Los morteros usados suelen ser el yeso, en interiores, y de cal y arena o cemento Portland en exteriores. La mezcla en los morteros de arenas no lavadas o procedentes de medios salinos es una fuente de problemas. También puede disminuir el agarre el uso de áridos no angulosos. El cemento Portland, por su parte, sustituto de los morteros naturales desde su invención por J. Aspdin en 1828, es uno de los grandes enemigos de la conservación debido a que produce sales alcalinas, entre ellas el sulfato de sodio. Otro problema puede presentarse en los cementos armados, ya que la formación de carbonatos de calcio en la masa, a lo largo del tiempo, hace que ésta pase de básica (Ph 12,5) a alcalina (Ph 8,5), provocando la corrosión de los mallazos y con ello fisuras en las estructuras de soporte (Fiorentini y Fiorentini, 2001).

Cuando la conservación del bien se ve comprometida por la presencia de patologías es necesario establecer un claro diagnóstico del inmueble y de su problemática, incluyendo la de los elementos aplicados, su naturaleza y los posibles factores de alteración que afectan a su conservación con la finalidad de erradicar las causas de éstos (Coll, 2001). El aspecto más problemático, sin embargo, es el criterio de intervención. Antoni González y su equipo de la Diputación de Barcelona han desarrollado una gran experiencia en la restauración de arquitecturas modernistas que incorporan el trencadís (González, 1993, 2006; González et al., 1994, 1995; Lacuesta, 1993, 2006).

En aportaciones previas indicábamos que en la arquitectura como un todo (estructuras, espacios y calidades aportadas por los múltiples elementos de diferentes materiales que se sustentan sobre ella), se plantea esencialmente el problema de la incapacidad de los componentes no estructurales de resolver el reto técnico de pervivencia que se les exige, ya que su papel arquitectónico es en muchos casos, además del decorativo, el de protección o complemento de la obra viva. Sin embargo, el hecho de su incapacidad de supervivencia es accidental en la mayor parte de los casos, y su alteración y substitución no son factores que fueran tenidos en cuenta por los creadores que los integraron en sus obras. Su fin se debe a las carencias de la propia arquitectura, a la falta de mantenimiento, a las patologías constructivas, a las bajas especificaciones del material aportado por la tecnología de su época y, evidentemente, a los avatares humanos que provocan y no solucionan esos problemas a lo largo del tiempo. El conservador/restaurador del monumento arquitectónico se enfrenta por todo ello a una situación compleja, ya que muchos de esos elementos llegan como restos, dificultando la comprensión de toda la obra, pero son, sin embargo, un importantísimo material con valor documental esencial para conocer aspectos de otros tiempos consubstanciales con la obra a preservar.

En el caso de cualquier actuación de conservación-restauración nos encontraremos con situaciones de mayor o menor complejidad administrativa derivada del nivel de protección jurídica del inmueble. No todas las arquitecturas poseen protección patrimonial, ni ésta abarca los mismos aspectos en función de su consideración, sea bajo una protección urbanística determinada, generalmente diferenciada en niveles (de menor a mayor: elementos singulares concretos, fachada y elementos básicos o, finalmente, protección integral), que pueden derivar en los casos más exigentes en su declaración como Bien de Relevancia Local o Bien de Interés Cultural. Las declaraciones específicas, en especial las de mayor nivel, requieren en su caso la redacción de un Plan Director que delimite las posibilidades de actuación sobre el inmueble. En éstos cabe plantear cuáles serían las directrices generales de las actuaciones de conservación y establecer los protocolos oportunos para que los responsables de las intervenciones supieran cómo organizar la necesaria supervisión multidisciplinar bajo la tutela de la Administración competente.

No existe una guía de soluciones universales en la restauración-conservación de edificios. Sí existe, sin embargo, un consenso sobre que cada caso debe tratarse de forma única y cada intervención debe regirse por metodologías específicas y por criterios consensuados por equipos pluridisciplinares (Coll, 2003). Poseemos un ya numeroso corpus de experiencias y es posible evaluar cuál ha sido el comportamiento y el resultado de estas intervenciones con cierta perspectiva (Coll et al., 1995; Coll, 1996, 1998; Alva et al., 2003).

Como proponíamos en el seminario ICCROM de Roma, la única vía para la comprensión de significados y toma de decisiones de cara a la intervención monumental deberá ser el trabajo multidisciplinar, el cual aportará las directrices a seguir. Ante la magnitud del problema no es posible plantear soluciones universales a modo de recetario, sin embargo consideramos que una serie de principios esenciales deben tenerse en cuenta a la hora de intervenir en el patrimonio arquitectónico:

1. Principio de la unidad de contexto. Se fundamenta en la práctica de la conservación *in situ*, la cual debe ser, a nuestro modo de ver, un condicionante fundamental a considerar, y regir la intervención garantizando lo máximo posible la salvaguardia de la materialidad auténtica de todos los bienes integrados en la arquitectura, ya que en sí mismos aportan una valiosa documentación histórica y patrimonial. Según la ley 16/1985 del Patrimonio Histórico Español que refrenda este principio, todos los bienes integrantes de la arquitectura tienen la consideración de bien inmueble ligada a su contenedor.
2. Principio de la salvaguardia del bien mueble. Cuando preservar el bien original *in situ* no es posible, quizás en ocasiones por la propia materialidad del objeto o por su naturaleza extemporánea al ser considerado una anécdota temporal no consubstancial al bien patrimonial, ese bien puede convertirse en objeto mueble. Su valor patrimonial no es por ello menor, ya que incluso fuera de contexto y con la documentación pertinente es un bien patrimonial esencial para la comprensión del monumento. Por ello consideramos irrenunciable la conservación preventiva del bien en instituciones especializadas de reconocida solvencia, evidentemente museos, colecciones museográficas o en el propio monumento gestionado con herramientas y personal competente y oportuno, todo ello regido por un Plan Director claro. Cualquier extracción de ese bien y apropiación privada o su abandono fuera de esos parámetros constituye un acto de expolio que empobrece la comprensión del monumento.
3. Principio de la «autenticidad». El principio de la autenticidad va unido por una parte al de la materialidad del bien. Esa materialidad depende de su tiempo, de la tecnología y conocimientos del momento de su producción. El hecho es especialmente sensible en la cerámica ya que es un material que ha evolucionado y que ha aportado en cada época bienes de naturaleza diferente. Por otra parte la autenticidad afecta a la capacidad de transmisión de los valores visuales táctiles, texturales y cromáticos de cada evento histórico. Entiendo que esta autenticidad, además, debe responder a las necesidades de nuestro tiempo, es decir, debe realizarse siguiendo las recomendaciones de la UNESCO y de las diversas Cartas del Restauro que se han preocupado del problema de posibilidad de reconocimiento del original respecto de lo añadido, sin renunciar por ello a aportar al monumento las soluciones del presente mediante nuevos materiales facilitados por nuestra tecnología. Por ello, completar suelos o revestimientos con elementos reproducidos artesanalmente según modelos del pasado puede ser un error en función de las especificaciones

exigibles al material. La conservación preventiva tiene su lenguaje, en el que la preservación del original es esencial. La restauración posee otras connotaciones de recuperación del bien original en donde, una vez preservados los elementos remanentes del pasado, se nos exige una intervención que permita la perduración futura del bien, siendo necesario para ello la mejor solución técnica.

4. Principio del mantenimiento. Es éste esencial en toda obra como primer criterio de conservación preventiva. En este campo de actuación se hace necesaria la formación específica de profesionales de conservación y restauración de bienes del patrimonio histórico tanto como la de profesionales de la arquitectura, ya que el correcto mantenimiento de la arquitectura en su estanqueidad, estabilidad estructural, etc. es el único procedimiento para su pervivencia integral.

En cuanto a la problemática concreta del trencadís, cabría hacer unas indicaciones sobre las posibilidades de su tratamiento en función de su estado, aunque en último término es el equipo pluridisciplinar rector de cada intervención quien debe decidir la solución a adoptar en cada caso.

— Debilidad, desintegración o desplazamiento de la masa de agarre con amenaza de desprendimiento de la decoración cerámica: existen varias posibilidades de intervención. Si es posible consolidar la masa de agarre es la solución más indicada. Si no fuera posible, debe considerarse la extracción del recubrimiento cerámico en masa manteniendo su geometría original. Tras su limpieza total y consolidación, debe prepararse un mortero adecuado para volver a recolocar el elemento.

— Pérdida de elementos de superficies decorativas. Es habitual que al darse el supuesto primero, o quizás por patologías del propio material utilizado en la decoración, se haya perdido una parte de ésta por caída de piezas. Debe evaluarse si el volumen de la pérdida permite una reconstrucción decorativa para devolver el cromatismo y el acabado original. Antes que dejar lagunas sin recubrir considero más interesante ocuparlas con materiales actuales que permiten una diferenciación entre lo preservado y lo nuevo, y ello tanto por motivos de comprensión del contexto original como por aspectos de conservación preventiva. No considero oportuno usar materiales antiguos para consolidaciones actuales dado que se puede producir mixtificaciones aunque sean bienintencionadas. El uso de documentación fotográfica previa (si existe) y el estudio de formas, texturas y colores es fundamental para aproximarse lo más posible al bien perdido en la reconstrucción de lagunas.

— Desintegración cromática y alteración de los elementos de superficies decorativas. En el caso de la erosión superficial por patologías provocadas por sales o ataques biológicos, con pérdidas cromáticas y de superficies vítreas, el elemento resultante, aún siendo en parte original, debe considerarse perdido en función del concepto que lo seleccionó originalmente. No conserva su aspecto original y mantenerlo en su ubicación en esas condiciones dificulta la compresión del monumento. Debería considerarse su conservación descontextualizada y su reposición tratando las partes alteradas como lagunas del caso anterior.

En cualquier caso, como ya han dicho muchos especialistas en numerosas ocasiones, no existe un recetario universal. Cada restauración debe mantener el método y la evaluación previa como criterio universal y partiendo de ello decidir la solución a adoptar (González, 1993; 2003; Coll, 2003). Soluciones técnicas y experiencia en conservación de materiales cerámicos *in situ* existen con profusión (Perla, 1990, 1993, 1995a, 1995b, 1996; Riu, 1989; Soberats, 1996; Ferrer Morales, 2007), incluso fuera de su contexto original (Coll et al., 2001; Rallo, 2001; Sanz, 2001; Torrijos, 2001; Carrascosa, 2006), pero creo que hay que defender una idea fundamental: el mejor lugar para la preservación de un elemento patrimonial estético es el que fue concebido para exhibirlo.

Epílogo

Esplendor y degradación del trencadís

Las formas fragmentadas y coloridas del trencadís gaudiniano, y aún más si se combinan con bordes redondeados, se han convertido en un elemento identificable al instante que nos remite a la imagen de Barcelona. Cabría preguntarse por qué el trencadís —y, de manera muy especial, el dragón-salamandra del Park Güell— se ha convertido en un icono de la ciudad. Barcelona tiene un pasado esplendoroso y un patrimonio medieval único. De hecho, hemos dedicado este libro, precisamente, a demostrar que la técnica del trencadís, aunque se partía de algunas experiencias ya existentes, no fue utilizada de manera regular hasta la década de 1880. ¿Cómo puede ser que Gaudí y el trencadís hayan adquirido esta indiscutible primacía entre los viajeros, pero también entre los propios vecinos de Barcelona? No es fácil dar respuestas más allá de un hecho que es indiscutible: la belleza de esta técnica musiva. Y de un segundo factor no menos importante, la sonoridad de la propia denominación: «trencadís».

Ante la incapacidad de entender las razones de esta realidad, nos proponemos hacer un recorrido a través de las nuevas creaciones que, en última instancia, no dejan de ser una muestra de los gustos cambiantes de la postmodernidad. Veremos, por un lado, piezas inspiradas en el color y la fragmentación gaudiniana, que han alcanzado un grado de creatividad muy innovadora, junto a la mercancía que llena los comercios de la ciudad, desde las boutiques más exclusivas o las selectas tiendas de museos, hasta los quioscos o los centros de *souvenirs*. Incluso, como protagonistas de la marca Barcelona, encontramos en los aeropuertos objetos de trencadís, entre camisetas con el nombre de la ciudad, peluches disfrazados de futbolistas y toda clase de bibelots, que ofrecen la última oportunidad al visitante para llevar a casa un objeto que caracterice a la ciudad.

Esta consideración es de hecho un tema recurrente en el marco del proceso artístico, la relación ambigua entre una obra de arte —producto de un tiempo y lugar determinados— y su reinterpretación posterior bajo diferentes condiciones culturales, en otro lugar y tiempo. La riqueza original y creativa del trencadís de Gaudí ha inspirado a muchos artistas, arquitectos y diseñadores, que han tomado la técnica como punto de partida del curso creativo, en un proceso muy alejado de la simple copia o interpretación. El pistoletazo de salida lo dio Joan Miró con su colaboración con Josep Llorens i Artigas en el espléndido mural de refractario del aeropuerto de Barcelona, en 1970, siguiendo un proyecto que ambos artistas habían iniciado en el Palacio de la UNESCO en París, (1957-1958). En estas obras se partía aún de una factura de piezas regular, pero ya en la escultura *Mujer y Pájaro* (1981-1982) —en este caso con la colaboración de Joan Gardy i Artigas—, situada en el parque del Escorxador, el revestimiento cerámico de la piedra artificial tiene toda la aparente improvisación del trencadís.

Pero fue en torno a la organización de los Juegos Olímpicos de 1992 que, como ya hemos señalado alguna otra vez (Freixa, Saliné, 2016), el color entró en la vida pública con grandes conjuntos escultóricos o instalaciones como la propuesta de Beverly Pepper, *Cielo caído*, en el jardín de la Estación del Norte (1988-1992), con las gradaciones tonales de color azul y blanco; la popular *Cara de Barcelona* (1992) de Roy Lichtenstein y Diego Delgado i Rajado; o la *Fuente Castellana* (1992), en la que la ceramista Madola (Maria Àngels Domingo i Laplana) contrapone baldosas de cerámica amarillas y blancas con el negro y azul del agua de otras baldosas. Unas últimas, y muy significativas muestras de trencadís, son la cubierta del Mercado de Santa Caterina (2005), donde Enric Miralles y Benedetta Tagliabue, con el ceramista e ingeniero Toni Cumella i Vendrell, traducen este modelo a una escala gigantesca; y el Auditorio de Tenerife (2003) y el Palau de les Arts Reina Sofía (2005), en Valencia, obras ambas de Santiago Calatrava, recubiertas de trencadís blanco. No obstante, señalaremos, como hecho curioso, que no encontramos en la producción actual de escultura de pequeñas dimensiones una referencia tan explícita a los modelos gaudinianos.

En otra escala, la del pequeño objeto de diseño o de objetos decorativos, hay una producción extensísima, manteles, bolígrafos, lápices y material de escritura, camisetas, imanes de nevera y similares que gravitan entre el papel de ser pequeños y diferentes recuerdos para los turistas —es el caso de las piedras pintadas a mano de Ann Swinnen de la «Colección Gaudí», que produjeron hace unos años las monjas del convento de Sant Benet, en Montserrat—, o las que tienen tantas empresas de diseño textil o de productos alimenticios, como el *Chocolate Blanco Trencadís*, creado por el chocolatero barcelonés Enric Rovira, el packaging de trencadís de la también empresa de chocolates barcelonesa Cacao Sampaka, o la cápsula Nespresso que, según su publicidad: «nuestro objetivo era encontrar un elemento representativo de Barcelona que, al mismo tiempo, se convirtiera en un icono de la marca». Un tono diferente tiene la producción de porcelanas Serra de objetos de regalo exclusivos con acabados de mucha calidad. Podemos encontrar otros objetos domésticos textiles, una marca de botellas de cava, o el modelo de la moto «Scoopy Gaudí»; y en el campo del diseño gráfico, algunas alusiones en los cartones de leche ATO, en cajas de bombones de Nestlé, y una innumerable variedad de cosas que han encontrado su camino en nuestra vida diaria. Hay que tener cuidado, sin embargo, tanto con la calidad de las técnicas utilizadas como en la coherencia del diseño del objeto, porque la línea entre la ironía y el ridículo es muy delgada.

De hecho, la mayoría de la producción reciente esconde detrás del trencadís un intento de dignificar obras de dudoso mérito estético. Este es el caso de aquellas empresas constructoras que se especializan en «recrear» la técnica del trencadís en instalaciones de gusto artístico cuestionable, como el dragón —parodia del del Park Güell— que aparece en el estanque del parque de Eliana de Valencia. Ciertamente, la mayoría de las versiones modernas que llenan las tiendas de recuerdos caen claramente dentro de la categoría de lo vulgar o kitsch. Un ejemplo que nos viene a todos a la memoria, porque satura todas las tiendas del centro de la ciudad, es el toro *Mosaico Gaudí Bull*, que vale 35 € y que, además de confundir realidades culturales totalmente alejadas, también ignora que Gaudí fue probablemente un adversario decidido de las corridas de toros. El toro tiene otros compañeros, una flamenca de trencadís y un cerdito rosa alado, el *Pig with wings Barcino*. Hemos encontrado también, y como objeto de lujo, una de las aceiteras que no gotea de Rafael Marquina —un moderno diseño clásico de Cataluña—, con un acabado esmaltado que imita el trencadís; y la lista sería interminable.

Sin embargo, todos los artículos anteriores, ya sea una caja de bombones, una taza de té, etc., tienen una cualidad en común: nos evocan la salamandra del Park Güell. Son más que un recuerdo, acaban siendo una metáfora de la ciudad.

Cited bibliography

ALMAGRO, A.; BESTUÉ, I.; BORRELLI, E. (2001): Preliminary session of *El Estudio y Conservación sobre cerámica decorada aplicada a la arquitectura.* Roma: ICCROM-Academia de España en Roma.

ALTÉS, F.X.; BARAUT, A.; GALOBART, J. (2013): *Antoni Gaudí a Montserrat.* Barcelona: Publicacions de l'Abadia de Montserrat.

ALTISENT, A. (1974): *Història de Poblet.* Poblet: Abadia de Poblet.

ALVA, A.; ALMAGRO, A.; BESTUÉ, I. (2003): *El estudio y la conservación de la Cerámica Decorada. Arquitectura.* Roma: ICCROM-Academia de España en Roma.

AMADOR de los RÍOS, R. (1915): "Reliquias de los Musulmanes en Cataluña", in *Revista de Archivos, Bibliotecas y Museos,* No. 9-12, p. 172-212. Madrid.

BASSEGODA, J. (1974): "Las conversaciones de Gaudí con Juan Bergós" in *Hogar y Arquitectura* No. 112, p. 50. Madrid.

BASSEGODA, J. (1978): *El Jardín de las Hespérides.* Madrid: Academia de San Fernando.

BASSEGODA, J. (1986): "The Inscriptions on the Bench at Park Güell as Trascribed by Joan Matamala i Flotats in 1967" in *Sites,* No. 15, p. 12-23. New York.

BASSEGODA, J. (1989): *El Gran Gaudí.* Sabadell: Ausa.

BASSEGODA, J. (2003): *Josep Bayó, contractista de Gaudí.* Barcelona: Edicions UPC.

BERGÓS i MASSÓ, J., *Gaudí, l'home i l'ombra.* Barcelona: Ariel, 1954. Modern edition (1999). Lumberg.

BOSCH, M.; OLONA, J. (2017): "Gaudí, Batlló, Nolla. Anécdota o voluntat", in *II Congreso Nacional sobre cerámica Nolla.* Unpublished.

BUENACASA, C. (2006): *Mosaicos Romanos de Siria, pintura en piedra.* Barcelona: Fundació arqueològica Clos.

CARRASCOSA, B. (2006): *Iniciación a la conservación y restauración de objetos cerámicos.* Valencia: Universidad Politécnica de Valencia.

CASAMARTINA, J. (2017): *Un Palau dins d'un altre.* Barcelona: Diputació de Barcelona.

CASANELLES, E. (1965): *Nueva visión de Gaudí.* Barcelona: La Polígrafa.

CASANOVA, R. (2002): "Gaudí i els seus col·laboradors: artistes i industrials a l'entorn del 1900" in *Gaudí 2002. Miscel·lània,* ed. BOHIGAS, O.; GIRALT-MIRACLE, D.; CASANOVA, R.,Barcelona: Planeta, Ajuntament de Barcelona.

CASANOVA, R. (2002): "Lluís Domènech i Montaner, a la recerca de la ceràmica moderna" in *Millars, espai i història* 2002, vol. 25, p. 155-173. Castellón de la Plana: Universitat Jaume I.

COLL, J. (1996): "Recientes intervenciones de restauración de azulejería en arquitectura en España", in *XI Congreso de Conservación y Restauración de Bienes Culturales.* Castellón de la Plana.

COLL, J. (1998): "Recubrimientos cerámicos en arquitectura. La problemática de su conservación en Valencia", in *Actas Qualicer'98, V Congreso Mundial de la calidad del azulejo y del pavimento cerámico, tom. II. Conferencias generales y Ponencias,* p. 101-111. Castellón de la Plana: Cámara Oficial de Comercio, Industria y Navegación.

COLL, J. (2001): "Teoría y filosofía de la intervención en restauración de revestimientos cerámicos en Arquitectura", in ALMAGRO, A.; BESTUÉ, I.; BORRELLI, E., Preliminary session of *El Estudio y Conservación sobre cerámica decorada aplicada a la arquitectura.* Roma: ICCROM-Academia de España en Roma.

COLL, J. (2003): "Reflexiones en torno a la conservación de la cerámica aplicada a la arquitectura", in ALVA, A.; ALMAGRO, A.; BESTUÉ, I., *El Estudio y la Conservación de la Cerámica Decorada en Arquitectura. Un compendio de colaboraciones,* p. 95-98. Roma: ICCROM-Academia de España en Roma.

COLL, J. (2008): *La cerámica valenciana.* Valencia: Asociación de cerámica valenciana.

COLL, J.; PÉREZ, J.; SCHUTZ, I. (Coord.) (1995): *Rehabilitación de la azulejería en la arquitectura,* p. 223. Alicante: Asociación de Ceramología.

COLL, J.; SANZ, M.; RALLO, C. (2001): *El azulejo en el Museo. Su conservación, restauración y montaje expositivo.* Madrid: Museo Nacional de Cerámica, Ministerio de Cultura.

DOMÈNECH I MONTANER, Ll. (1903): "L'Antoni Ma. Gallissà en l'intimitat", in *La Veu de Catalunya,* (21-05-1903). Barcelona.

DURÁN, M. (2006): "La cerámica del Banco del Park Güell (1909-1914)", in Asociación de Ceramología, *Tradición y Modernidad: La cerámica en el Modernismo, IX Congreso Anual de la Asociación de Ceramología,* p. 81-98. Barcelona: Ajuntament d'Esplugues de Llobregat, Universitat de Barcelona.

FANNELLI, G.; GARGIANI, R. (1999): *El principio del revestimento. Prolegómenos a una Historia de la Arquitectura Contemporánea.* Madrid: Akal.

FANCELLI, P. (2003): "L'invetriatura fra archittetura e restauro" in ALVA, A.; ALMAGRO, A.; BESTUE, I., *El Estudio y la Conservación de la Cerámica Decorada en Arquitectura. Un compendio de colaboraciones,* p. 52-57. Roma: ICCROM-Academia de España en Roma.

FARINHA, JL.; SOUSA, D. (2003): "The removal and replacing of architectural glazed tiles - azulejos. A case study", in ALVA, A.; ALMAGRO, A.; BESTUE, I., *El Estudio y la Conservación de la Cerámica Decorada en Arquitectura. Un compendio de colaboraciones,* p. 22-27. Roma: ICCROM-Academia de España en Roma.

FERRER, A. (2014): *La cerámica arquitectónica: su conservación y restauración.* Sevilla: Universidad de Sevilla, Secretariado de Publicaciones.

FIORENTINI, I.; FIORENTINI, E. (2001): *Mosaico. Materiali, Tecniche e Storia.* Ravenna: MWeV Editore.

FLORES, C. (1974): "Algunas precisiones sobre la figura y la obra de J.M. Jujol" in *La arquitectura de J.M. Jujol.* Barcelona: COAC, La Gaya Ciencia.

FLORES, C. (2002): *Les lliçons de Gaudí.* Barcelona: Empúries.

FREIXA, M.; LENIZ, M.: *El Park Güell.* Museu d'Història de Barcelona, in press.

GAUDÍ, A.: *Antoni Gaudí. Manuscritos, artículos, conversaciones y dibujos.* Murcia: Colegio Oficial de Aparejadores y arquitectos técnicos, 1982, (editor by Marcià Codinachs).

GAUDÍ, A.: *Escritos y documentos.* Barcelona: El Acantilado, 2002, (editor by Laura Mercader).

GALI, D.; LACUESTA, R.; MICALÓ, M. (2004): "Atles del material decoratiu de ceràmica i vidre de l'església de la Colònia Güell" in *Quaderns científics i tècnics de restauració monumental,* No. 14, p. 163-196. Barcelona: Institut d'Edicions de la Diputació de Barcelona.

GONZÁLEZ, A. (1993): "La restauración del Palau Güell: criterios y actitudes" in *Quaderns Científics i Tècnics,* No. 5, p. 217-230. Barcelona: Diputació de Barcelona.

GONZÁLEZ, A.; CARBÓ, P. (1994): *Restauración del Palau Güell de Barcelona.* Barcelona: Diputació de Barcelona, Área de Cooperació, Servei de Patrimoni Arquitectònic Local.

GONZÁLEZ, A. (2003): "Tradition, modernity, synthesis glazed ceramics in architecture", in ALVA, A.; ALMAGRO, A.; BESTUÉ, I., *El Estudio y la Conservación de la Cerámica Decorada en Arquitectura. Un compendio de colaboraciones,* p. 58-63. Roma: ICCROM-Academia de España en Roma.

GONZÁLEZ MARTÍ, M. (1952): "La azulejería medieval valenciana (1238-1500)" in *Cerámica del Levante español. Siglos medievales. Tomo III, Alicatados y azulejos.* Barcelona.

GONZÁLEZ, A.; LACUESTA, R. (2013): *El Palacio Güell. Una obra maestra de Antoni Gaudí.* Barcelona: Diputació de Barcelona.

GUEILBURG, L. (2002): “L’argila, material original de l’arquitectura de Gaudí” in *La ceràmica a l’obra de Gaudí*. Barcelona: Centre d’Estudis Gaudinistes, Col·legi d’Aparelladors i Arquitectes Tècnics de Catalunya.

GRISET, J. (2015): *L’art del Mosaic hidràulic a Catalunya*. Barcelona: Ajuntament de Barcelona, Viena Edicions.

JUJOL, J. Mª junior. (1974): “Jujol, un artista completo” in *La arquitectura de J. Mª Jujol*, Barcelona: COAC, La Gaya Ciencia.

LACUESTA, R. (1993). “Análisis artístico y constructivo: las chimeneas de la azotea del Palau Güell” in *Quaderns Científics i Tècnics*, No. 5, p. 237-242. Barcelona: Diputació de Barcelona.

LARA, F. (2000a): “La cerámica arquitectónica suntuaria del Antiguo Egipto”, in *La Ruta de la Cerámica*, p. 19-21. Zaragoza: Taller Escuela de Cerámica de Muel, Diputación de Zaragoza.

LARA, F. (2000b): “La cerámica arquitectónica suntuaria en Mesopotamia”, in *La Ruta de la Cerámica*, p. 22-25. Zaragoza: Taller Escuela de Cerámica de Muel, Diputación de Zaragoza.

LAUMAIN, X.; LÓPEZ, A. (1916): *El mosaico Nolla y la renovación de la cerámica industrial arquitectónica en Valencia*. Valencia: Editorial CIDCeN.

LUPERCIO, C. A. (2015): “Estudi històric i artístic *d’Hèrcules buscant les Hespèrides* i el seu pintor Aleix Clapés” in *D’Hèrcules buscant les Hespèrides*. Barcelona: Palau Güell, MNAC.

MATTA PUGA, C. (2003): “Sobre la conservación de los azulejos del Convento de San Francisco de Lima”, in ALVA, A.; ALMAGRO, A.; BESTUÉ, I., *El Estudio y la Conservación de la Cerámica Decorada en Arquitectura. Un compendio de colaboraciones*, p. 71-78. Roma: ICCROM-Academia de España en Roma.

MARTINELL, C. (1951): *Gaudí i la Sagrada Família*. Barcelona: Aymà.

MESA REDONDA (2006): “La restauración y conservación del patrimonio cerámico aplicado a la arquitectura”, in Asociación de Ceramología, *Tradición y Modernidad: La cerámica en el Modernismo, IX Congreso Anual de la Asociación de Ceramología*, p. 395-417. Barcelona: Ajuntament d’Esplugues de Llobregat, Universitat de Barcelona.

NAVARRO, I. (1993): *Masies de Les Corts: torres, masos i altres cases*. Barcelona: Ajuntament de Barcelona, Districte de Les Corts.

ONECHA, B.; BOSCH,M.; OLONA, J.; DOTOR, A. (2017): “Plan director de la Casa Batlló de Gaudí un antes y un después” in *ACE: Architecture, City and Environement (Arquitectura, Ciudad y Entorno)*, 11 (33), p. 65-86. Barcelona: Universitat Politècnica de Catalunya.

PERLA, A. (1990): “La cerámica” in VVAA, *Un monumento recuperado. La rehabilitación del Hospital de Jornaleros de Maudes*, p. 131-161. Madrid: Consejería de Política Territorial de la Comunidad Autónoma de Madrid.

PERLA, A. (1993): “Una compleja intervención. La recuperación de los zócalos de azulejería del Claustrillo de La Cartuja de Santa María de las Cuevas de Sevilla” in *Azulejo*, Revista del Museo Nacional do Azulejo, p. 74-92. Lisbon.

PERLA, A. (1995a): “Principios y criterios para la restauración de la cerámica aplicada a la arquitectura”, in COLL, et. al. (Coord.), *Rehabilitación de la azulejería en la arquitectura*. Asociación de Ceramología, august, p. 11-34. Barcelona.

PERLA, A. (1995b): “Sistemas mecánicos de arranque en azulejería: la Estación del Vasco -Oviedo- y la Cartuja de Sevilla”, in COLL, et. al. (Coord.), *Rehabilitación de la azulejería en la arquitectura*. Asociación de Ceramología, august, p. 103-134. Barcelona.

PERLA, A. (1996). “La restauración de las fachadas del Palacio de Velázquez de Madrid” in *Qualicer 96*, II, p. 509-524. Castellón de la Plana.

RÀFOLS, JF.; FALGUERA, F. (1928): *Antoni Gaudí*. Barcelona: Canosa.

RALLO, C. (2001): “La restauración de los azulejos en el Museo Nacional de Cerámica”, in *El azulejo en el Museo. Su conservación, restauración y montaje expositivo*, p. 19-23. Madrid: Ministerio de Cultura, Museo Naciona l de Cerámica.

RAVAGNOLI, A.; KRAJEWSKI, A. (2003): "Stato della degradazione e ragioni del degrado: indagine chimico-fisiche e micro climatiche", in ALVA, A.; ALMAGRO, A.; BESTUÉ, I., *El Estudio y la Conservación de la Cerámica Decorada en Arquitectura. Un compendio de colaboraciones,* p. 28-37. Roma: ICCROM-Academia de España en Roma.

RIU DE MARTIN, C. (1989): "Ignasi Mayolas and the restoration of ceramics applied to architecture" in *Azulejos,* No. 58, p. 84-87.

RODRÍGUEZ, J. A.; SALINÉ, M. (2017): "El *trencadís* de Gaudí como método de expresión arquitectónica en la Ciudad de Cartagena", in *El Modernismo en el Arco Mediterráneo,* p. 359-368. Cartagena: Universidad Politécnica de Cartagena.

SALINÉ, M. (2005): *Lluís Brú, fragments d'un creador. Els mosaics modernistes.* Esplugues de Llobregat: Ajuntament d'Esplugues de Llobregat.

SALINÉ, M. (2015): *El mosaic modernista a Catalunya (1888-1929). De la mà de Lluís Brú i Salelles i l'obra de Lluís Domènech i Montaner.* Barcelona: Universitat de Barcelona, GRACMON.

SANZ, M. (2001): "Sistemas de soportes para la exposición de azulejos", in *El azulejo en el Museo. Su conservación, restauración y montaje expositivo,* p. 13-18. Madrid: Ministerio de Cultura, Museo Nacional de Cerámica.

SCHWARZ, H.J.; FREYBURG, S.; MOTTNER, P.; STADLBAUER, E. (2003): "Conservation and restoration of glazed architectural ceramics in northern Germay", in ALVA, A.; ALMAGRO, A.; BESTUÉ, I., *El Estudio y la Conservación de la Cerámica Decorada en Arquitectura. Un compendio de colaboraciones,* p. 38-41. Roma: ICCROM-Academia de España en Roma.

SOBERATS, F. (1995): "Criterios de intervención en el Gran Hotel de Palma de Mallorca", in COLL, et. al. (Coord.), *Rehabilitación de la azulejería en la arquitectura.* Asociación de Ceramología, august, p. 53-72. Barcelona.

SOLÍS BURGOS, J. A. (2003): "La restauración de la cerámica vidriada de la Plaza de España, Sevilla", in ALVA, A.; ALMAGRO, A.; BESTUÉ, I., *El Estudio y la Conservación de la Cerámica Decorada en Arquitectura. Un compendio de colaboraciones,* p. 42-45. Roma: ICCROM-Academia de España en Roma.

SUBÍAS, P. (2000): "La cerámica arquitectónica en Cataluña", in Taller-Escuela de Cerámica de Muel, *La Ruta de la Cerámica,* p. 155-170. Zaragoza: Diputación Provincial.

SUBÍAS, P. (2006): "Pujol i Bausis. Una empresa cerámica en el Modernismo", in Asociación de Ceramología, *Tradición y Modernidad: La cerámica en el Modernismo, IX Congreso Anual de la Asociación de Ceramología,* p. 217-254. Barcelona: Ajuntament d'Esplugues de Llobregat, Universitat de Barcelona.

SUBIAS, P. (2016): "La cerámica arquitectónica y la baldosa hidráulica en Bellesguard, transmisoras del pensamiento de Gaudí", in *Gaudí 2nd World Congress.* Barcelona. Unpublished.

TORRIJOS, E. (2001): "Proceso de restauración", in *El azulejo en el Museo. Su conservación, restauración y montaje expositivo,* p. 35-43. Madrid: Ministerio de Cultura, Museo Nacional de Cerámica.

VALL, J. Mª. (2014): *Bell Esguard. De la residència de Martí l'Humà a la Torre de Gaudí.* Barcelona: Ajuntament de Barcelona, Editorial Duxelm.

VENDRELL, M. (2003): "Cerámica decorada en la arquitectura. Degradación, patologías e investigación aplicada", in ALVA, A.; ALMAGRO, A.; BESTUÉ, I., *El Estudio y la Conservación de la Cerámica Decorada en Arquitectura. Un compendio de colaboraciones,* p. 10-14. Roma: ICCROM-Academia de España en Roma.

VOCCOLI, O. (2009): *La rinascita dell'arte musiva in epoca moderna in Europa. La tradizione del mosaico in Italia, in Spagna e in Inghliterra.* Barcelona: Universitat de Barcelona, GRACMON.

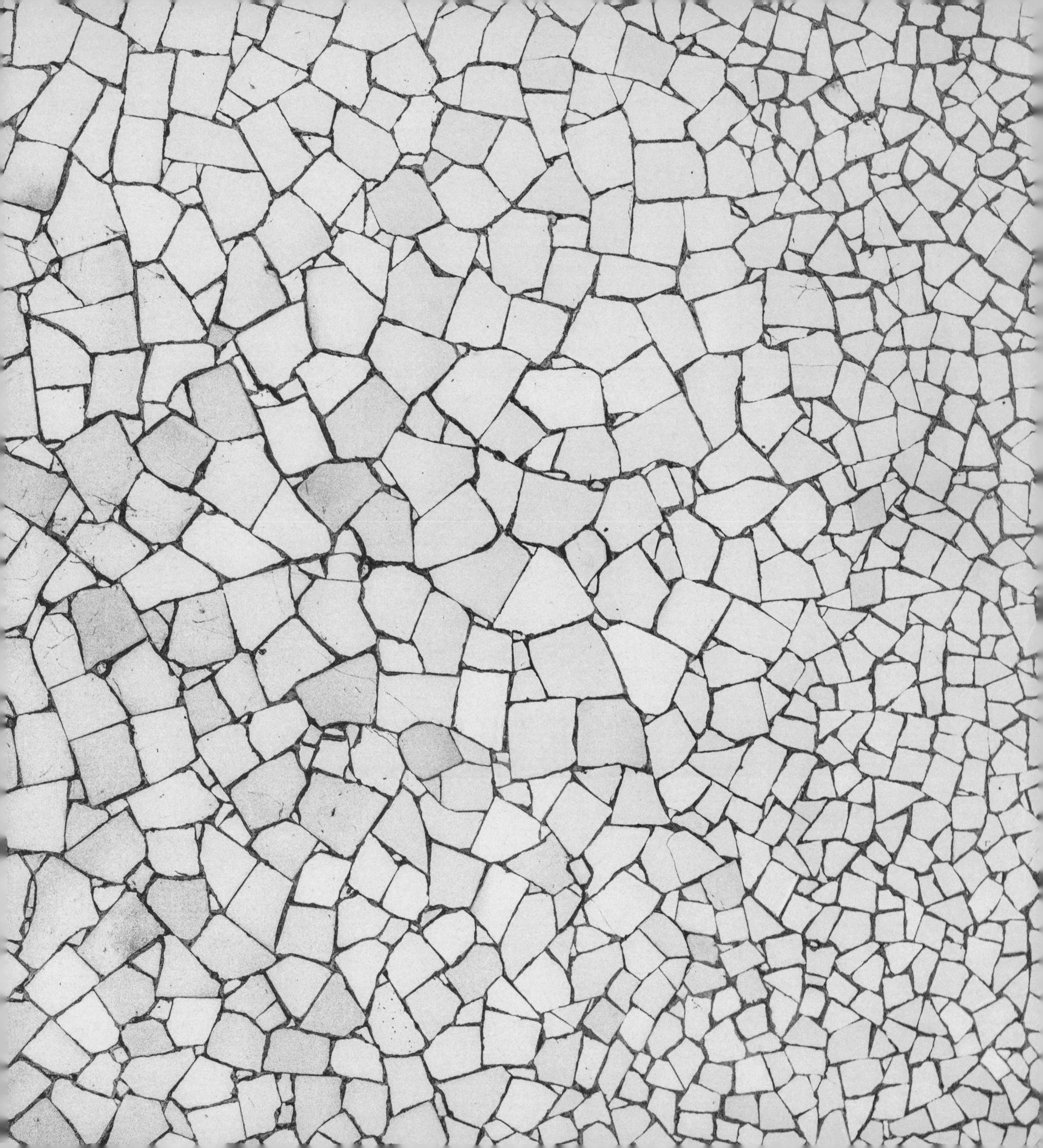